BREAKING FREE
WHO DEFEATS WHOM

Branden: Alfred, think about this. What is your estimate of people who resent intelligence? What is your estimate of people who resent a boy who ask questions? Who wants to understand things? Who won't accept things blindly on faith? What is your estimate of people who want to crush you because you can think? Who want to make you feel guilty because you can think?

Alfred: I'd like to get some whore and screw her in church.

Branden: Don't you see? You have made them your masters—your mother and father, the priest, everybody who hurt you. Everybody you have to defy. You are a puppet, and they are pulling the strings. Only it is in reverse. Instead of doing everything they want you to do, you do everything they don't want you to do. But it is still these people who are controlling you. It isn't your desires that motivate you—it's theirs. Theirs, turned backwards. They tell you you are evil, so to defy them, you do things that cause you to despise them, you do things that cause you to despise yourself. And so you fall into their trap. Who wins? Who defeats whom?

Alfred: I feel like I'm going to explode.

BREAKING FREE
Nathaniel Branden

BANTAM BOOKS
TORONTO • NEW YORK • LONDON • SYDNEY

BREAKING FREE

*A Bantam Book / published by arrangement with
Nash Publishing Corporation*

PRINTING HISTORY

Nash edition published November 1970

Bantam edition / December 1972
2nd printing .. *December 1972*   3rd printing ...... *August 1973*
4th printing .... *July 1981*

ISBN 0–553–20330–4

Published simultaneously in the United States and Canada

PRINTED IN THE UNITED STATES OF   AMERICA

13 12 11 10 9 8 7 6 5 4

FOREWORD

This is not a book I ever expected to write.

On the morning of the day I decided to write it, my mind was occupied with a different book entirely, one I had been planning for some time, that was to follow *The Psychology of Self-Esteem.*

When I finished *The Psychology of Self-Esteem* and saw it through publication, in 1969, it was the completion of a task that had dominated my existence for seven years: the delineation of a new concept of man's psychological nature, and an analysis of the meaning and consequences of man's need of self-esteem. In writing that book, my most general goal was to lay the foundation of a new system of psychology—and the foundation of any future book I would write.

Since that foundation is relevant to the present work, let me summarize, in briefest essentials, some of the central themes of *The Psychology of Self-Esteem.*

In that book, it was my purpose to establish:

that, since man's faculty of reason is his basic means of survival, the development of his mind, the development of his ability to think, is the foremost requirement of his well-being;

that, since the choice to think or not to think, to exercise his reason or to suspend it, is volitional, man is uniquely a self-determined and self-created being;

that, since man's emotions and desires are the product of conscious or subconscious value judgments, the premises, conclusions and values he arrives at or accepts, and with which he "programs" his subconscious, are essential to an explanation of his behavior;

that, since man's life depends on his cognitive contact with reality, the ability to achieve such contact, unobstructed by reality-avoiding blocks and distortions, is the necessary standard of mental health;

that, since man must achieve self-esteem by his own volitional effort—since man must make himself into an entity able to live (able to deal with reality efficaciously) and worthy of living (worthy of happiness)—his need of self-esteem is his need of the knowledge that he has succeeded at this task;

that, since self-esteem *is* a basic psychological need, the failure to achieve it leads to disastrous consequences and, in fact, underlies all neurotic disorders;

that, since a man's self-concept is crucially important to his choice of values and goals, the degree of his self-esteem (or lack of it) has a profound impact on his desires, his ambitions, his productive activity, his sexual-romantic responses, indeed on every aspect of his life.

A minor purpose of the book was to indicate the impoverishment and destructiveness of psychoanalysis and behaviorism—two schools that are in the forefront of the wave of the anti-intellectualism and irrationalism that dominates contemporary psychology.

Nine months after the book was completed, I began making notes for the next book, which was to explore in greater depth certain issues touched on only briefly in *The Psychology of Self-Esteem*. Then, one day, during one of my group therapy sessions, certain developments exploded in front of me—and before the night was over, I knew that I would have to drop everything and write this book.

It happened in the following way. . . .

CONTENTS

The Discovery of The Method 1
The Questions 11
The Unknowable 16
The Surrender 27
The Pressure Chamber 38
The Inheritance 46
The Barbarians 50
Annihilation 58
The Dreamers 67
Zero 74
The Sinner 85
Parental Love and Other Tragedies 99
The Gambler 106
Family Life 112
The Dropout 121
"We Poor Sinners" 129
Time Travel 138
Togetherness 146
Anti-Self 152
The Burdened 160
Contagion 167
Armor 176
The Shame Mongers 189
The End and The Beginning 196

Breaking Free is the second of three books that deal on different levels and from different perspectives with the role of self-esteem in human life. Each of these books is entirely independent and self-contained.

The first, *The Psychology of Self-Esteem*, is the most comprehensive and also the most technical of my works. It is, further, the most philosophical. It provides a detailed exploration of the facts of our nature, as psychological beings, that generates the need of self-esteem as well as establish the conditions of its fulfillment.

The Disowned Self, the third in the series, is in many respects a sequel to *The Psychology of Self-Esteem*. It represents something of a shift in emphasis from a purely cognitive aspect of self-esteem development toward a more detailed focus on feelings, emotions, and the problem of self-disowning and self-alienation. It also represents a more accurate portrayal of my approach to psychotherapy than do either of the other two books.

Breaking Free, the middle book in the series, is essentially a collection of brief case studies dealing with the childhood origins of negative self-concepts. I feel the need to mention that the therapeutic approach conveyed in these studies is very remote from my way of working today or for some years past—which in no way invalidates the psychological observations the study contains.

In my own estimation, *Breaking Free* is a very deceptive book: On one level, it is simply a collection of stories; on another, it is a succession of nightmares so appalling that the reader may not allow him-or-herself to experience fully the meaning of what is being presented; on another path still, it may become a path to self-liberation.

All of these books are available in Bantam editions, I am happy to say.

Nathaniel Branden
1981

The Discovery
of the Method

In addition to my work with clients on an individual basis, I conduct several group therapy sessions a week. One of these groups happens to consist almost exclusively of men; all are in their twenties, and all share certain problems: passivity, procrastination, lack of ambition, depression. They are all above average in intelligence.

One afternoon, I inquired of one of them if he had been raised in what I described as a "high-pressure" atmosphere: a home environment in which he constantly felt overwhelmed by expectations and demands concerning his performance which he felt inadequate to satisfy. Remarks he had made previously had suggested this avenue of approach to me. He answered rather emphatically in the affirmative—as did several other members of the group, speaking about themselves.

My reason for initiating this line of inquiry was the knowledge that children who feel overwhelmed by demands they cannot satisfy sometimes react with total passivity as their form of defense or of coping

1

with the intolerable. Without being consciously aware
of what they are doing, they in effect go on strike
psychologically; they do not argue with their parents,
they do not rebel openly, they accept verbal and
even physical abuse without complaining—they
merely retreat inwardly and do nothing. Unfortunately, this manner of responding to pressure often per-
sists long after the cause that precipitated it has
ceased to exist; so that, as adults, they find it extraor-
dinarily difficult to tolerate pressures or deadlines or
commitments of any kind; they are still fighting an
unresolved battle of childhood, and their method of
fighting that battle has become a way of life.

As I sat listening to members of the group recount
incidents of "high-pressure" expectations and demands to which they had been subjected, and with
which they had felt powerless to deal, I began to
notice—on the faces of men who predominantly were
very emotionally closed and repressed—growing indi-
cations of hurt, of anguish, of bewilderment and of
quietly intense rage.

I encouraged them to pay attention to the emotions
they were feeling and to let themselves experience
those emotions fully—not to block them or inhibit
them or repress them. I explained that it was healthy
and desirable to release those feelings, to bring them
into full conscious awareness. These were emotions
they had not permitted themselves to experience as
children; they had repressed them out of fear or
confusion or guilt or the desire to remain "in control."
I explained that repressed, stored-up pain always represents an unsolved problem; that such repression is
neither rational nor practical; and that only by feeling
the pain now, only by admitting and experiencing its
full reality, could one resolve the problem buried in
that pain. I explained that no pain was so destructive
as the pain one refuses to face—and no suffering so

enduring as the suffering one refuses to acknowledge.

When a person undergoes an experience that occasions profound suffering, his psychological well-being requires that he assimilate that experience, intellectually and emotionally, that he integrate it, that he deal with it consciously and rationally, so that he is not scarred by long-range harmful effects—such as the explicit or implicit conclusion that life is inherently tragic, that frustration and defeat are inevitable, that intimacy or fulfillment in human relationships is impossible, that happiness and self-esteem are unobtainable, that he is helpless or stupid or ineffectual or evil by nature. In repressing the pain occasioned by some shattering experience, a person forbids himself to know the meaning and significance that that experience has for him: the experience cannot be dealt with consciously and conceptually; it cannot be assimilated rationally and integrated non-self-destructively.

Implicit in the repression of pain is the conclusion: here is a problem with which I am helpless to deal. This conclusion paves the way for other devastating inferences, such as I have indicated above.

This, I explained to the group, is one of the main reasons why it is so important to derepress the memory and the pain of past traumatic events and experiences. It is important to bring into conscious awareness not merely the knowledge of what happened, but also the emotion one felt in response to what happened—in order to understand the exact value-significance that one attached to the experience, and the conclusion that one drew from it.

"But how," a young man asked, "can I derepress what I felt in those early years, when it's all blocked off, when I can't recall what I felt, when there is only a dim awareness ... like something I'm seeing from far away ... of some kind of heaviness inside me, feelings of misery I can't get to but I know are there?"

"That's what I want to know," said another participant in the group. "What I'd like is some advice, if you have any, some kind of guideline on how to break through—how to get in touch with what's down there, inside me—so that I can feel it, whatever it is."

"Christ, I've got a worse problem," said someone else. "You guys are talking about your difficulty in remembering your feelings. *But I can't even remember what happened.* I swear to God I've got amnesia, I've got amnesia for the first ten or eleven years of my life. It's a complete blank. So how can I know what I felt about events I don't even remember?"

Then, as I sat wondering how best to answer them, a complex chain of thought flashed through my mind. I recalled an incident typical of the kind I frequently encounter in the practice of private therapy, when it is necessary to teach a client how to identify repressed or hard-to-isolate feelings.

A woman came into the office with the following complaint: she loves her husband, she feels that he genuinely loves her, and she admires him enormously; but she is oppressed by some vague and undefinable pain, the sense of some nameless frustration that is having the effect of alienating her from her husband. As I groped for a clue to the cause of her problem, I ran through a mental checklist—a checklist derived from my knowledge of the elements that should be present in a love relationship between a man and a woman if the relationship is a good one.

I asked: "Does your husband's way of dealing with you and treating you have the effect of giving you an enhanced awareness of your own femininity?" I knew that, in a truly fulfilling romantic relationship, the answer to such a question is Yes. The woman looked astonished; it was a question that she had never thought of asking herself. She gazed into space, an expression of tension and sadness touching her eyes, and I knew that I had reached her. "No," she answered; she took a deep breath and went on: "As a matter of fact...." Now she was talking rapidly; she was stimulated, relevant facts and emotions were suddenly accessible to her conscious mind; and she began to speak about her frustrations—frustrations she was identifying for the first time in her life.

Recalling this incident, and other incidents of a similar kind, I thought: the method is to provide the question that will teach the client where to look; the method is to supply the category, to open the avenue of inquiry, to help the client to focus his or her attention in the appropriate direction....

Then I thought: I have a great many convictions about how children should be raised and about what parents can do to encourage the development of healthy self-esteem in their children. I also understand what mistakes parents can make. What if ...

I said to the group: "I'd like to try something. Please take out your notebooks. I am going to ask you a number of questions about the way in which your parents dealt with you and raised you. For the moment, just write down these questions. We will talk about them later."

I dictated a list of questions at random, as they occurred to me. When I had dictated perhaps ten questions, I noticed that several of my most stony-faced, repressed clients had tears in their eyes; the hands of some were shaking; others had mouths clamped tight or twisted into odd shapes. The boy who claimed to have amnesia for the first ten or eleven years of his life suddenly cried out: "Oh, God! What I'm remembering! The things that are coming back to me!"

I had found what I wanted.

The tension in the room, the emotional involvement, the excitement—and the pain—were overwhelming. Several people began to speak at once, their minds filled with memories of highly charged events—and emotions of bewilderment, of hurt, of uncomprehending fear and uncomprehending anger. It was one of the most productive sessions we had ever had.

That evening I was scheduled to work with another group. The evening group was more typical, in that it contained an approximately equal number of men and women, a wider range of ages and a greater diversity of problems.

When the group was assembled, I announced that we were going to perform an experiment. I said that I would begain by dictating a list of questions—questions about their childhood and their parents' manner of raising them—and that I merely wanted them to write down the questions. We would discuss their thoughts and reactions later.

I had had a chance to think about the contents of the list and to improve on the earlier version. I began to dictate the revised version.

It happened again.

It happened more violently this time. Tears in the eyes of clients who never cried. Anger on the faces of clients who never displayed anger. Hands trembling too much to write.

As the flood of repressed memories and emotions poured out, I encouraged my clients to focus on the content of their emotions, and to let themselves experience their emotions fully. I devoted the balance of the session to helping them identify as much as they could about the nature of their feelings. I knew that if I began the intricate process of intellectual analysis too soon, the memory of their childhood experiences would remain but the emotional impact of those experiences might be lost, might again be sub-merged.

I explained what our procedure was to be in work-ing with these questions. The first step was to answer the questions. The next, to cite examples in support of one's answers. Then, to attempt to describe exhaus-tively all the emotions that the memory of those examples invoked. The next, to answer the question: How were those emotions intellectually and emotion-ally handled in childhood? (Were they denied and repressed, were they "acted out" or what?) And final-ly, to take up the all important issue: What *conclu-sions* were drawn on the basis of those childhood experiences?

The conclusions they drew as children, I explained—conclusions about themselves, about other people, about life—were often made subverbally and implic-itly; but they were conclusions that nonetheless influ-enced behavior. And, often, they were retained into adulthood—unchecked, unexamined, unevaluated.

Did I mean to imply that all the important conclu-sions drawn in childhood, that affected their personal development, were drawn on the basis of experiences with their parents?

No, I did not; merely that crucial conclusions often are drawn in that context, and that this was an ave-nue of investigation clearly deserving of our atten-tion.

Did I mean to imply that human beings are the passive psychological products of the way in which their parents dealt with and raised them—that they are, in effect, their parents' psychological creation?

No, I did not. As I had explained in *The Psycholo-gy of Self-Esteem,* human beings are the product of the thinking they have done or have failed to do, and of the conclusions, premises and values that result from that thinking or nonthinking. I am not an advocate of environmental determinism; I am firmly opposed to that doctrine. But since a person's parents are usually his first encounter with the human race, his first experience of interaction with other human beings, it is not astonishing that crucially important premises are often formed in that context.

Did I mean to imply that a child necessarily *had* to draw the conclusions he did from his experiences with his parents?

No, I did not. Different children draw different conclusions from very similar experiences. Some children are much more mentally active than others in reflecting upon the meaning of the things they observe and the things that happen to them. But since it was already apparent that many members of the group had drawn disastrous conclusions on the basis of childhood experiences with their parents, it was obviously desirable for us to explore the nature of those conclusions and the reasons for them.

Did I mean to imply that any negative self-concepts or tragic attitudes toward life retained into adulthood necessarily had their origin in conclusions formed in the context of the child-parent relationship?

No, not necessarily. But, very often, they *are* formed in that context.

I concluded the session in a state of intense intellectual excitement. On the basis of the reactions my questions had elicited, there was no doubt that I had discovered a potent tool of therapeutic investigation. And more: listening to the accounts of childhood experiences, I felt that I had lifted the lid off hell—I had seen more vividly and clearly than ever before the full magnitude of the nightmare of most child-parent relations, the nightmare that is seldom recognized as such, because it is so common.

I thought: there is a book I must write about this, someday. . . .

That night, I could not sleep. I lay awake thinking about the questions, thinking about the responses they had elicited, thinking about the story that was crying to be told. By morning, I had reached the decision to write the book immediately.

It is my practice to have an assistant present at each of my group therapy sessions, taking almost verbatim notes on everything that transpires, everything that is said by me or by my clients. I have edited some of these notes for use in this book, in order to protect the privacy of my clients, to omit irrelevant interruptions or digressions, and to straighten out some of the grammar and syntax; in certain instances, I have amplified the meaning of statements that would not be clear without the context of preceding group discussions; in a few cases, I united two consecutive discussions with a client into one conversation. None of the names used are the names of actual clients. But aside from these details, the story I am to tell is recorded as it happened—as I worked through my list of questions with individual clients; as they and I discovered together a new method of self-exploration, a new method of tracing the childhood origins of negative self-concepts and a tragic or malevolent response to life.

Predictably, the questions were not equally productive with all clients—sometimes the childhood origins of their problems lay outside their relationship to their parents. But in no case did the line of inquiry to be presented prove less than illuminating; it was only a matter of degree.

The most dramatic conflicts are, perhaps, those that take place not between men but between a man and himself—where the arena of conflict is a solitary mind. I have always been keenly aware of the drama inherent in the therapeutic process, in the struggle between the client's desire to grow, to fulfill his human potential, and the subterranean forces of resistance and repression, generated by fear, pulling him downward. It was fascinating to observe this process, as I worked with my clients on my list of questions, to watch their struggle against repression, their efforts to think clearly despite acute suffering, their abrupt digressions into irrelevancies, triggered by panic, the too-hasty agreement aimed at ending the discussion before they were obliged to fully absorb and integrate what was being said, the sudden eruptions of emotional violence, the relapses into passivity and resignation, then the resurrection of their desire to fight, to break their chains, to burst free. That is the drama I invite the reader to share with me in the pages that follow.

Aside from my professional colleagues, to whom is this book addressed? It is addressed to anyone who is dissatisfied with the present level of his self-understanding—anyone who wishes to learn more about the steps by which his personality and psychological make-up came to be formed. It is addressed to every parent who does not want to become, or does not want to remain, a psychological destroyer.

I have said that this is a book I never expected to write. I had not foreseen that I would write a book that would deal, in this manner, with the psychological problems of children; nor a book that would be, in part and by implication, a primer on child-raising. But every therapist is and must be a child psychologist to some extent—if only because the child is still there, inside the neurotic adult whom we are treating. He is there, and he is screaming.

This is the story of what he is screaming about.

The Questions

As I presented the list of questions to my various groups, as well as to many of the clients whom I saw privately, I kept revising and improving the questions; I discovered which ones elicited the most productive and revealing responses. I found that sometimes different questions elicited essentially the same information. Here is the final version of my questions:

1. When you were a child, did your parents' manner of behaving and of dealing with you give you the impression that you were living in a world that was rational, predictable, intelligible? Or a world that was bewildering, contradictory, incomprehensible, unknowable?

2. Were you taught the importance of learning to think, the importance of developing your mind, the importance of becoming a rational being? Did your parents provide you with intellectual stimulation and convey the idea

11

that the use of your mind can be an exciting pleasure?

3. Were you encouraged to think independently, to develop your critical faculty? Or were you taught to be obedient rather than mentally active and questioning?

These *supplementary questions* were found, in many cases, to elicit the same response and the same information:

Did your parents project that it was more important to conform to what other people believed than to discover what is true?

When your parents wanted you to do something, did they appeal to your understanding and give you reasons for their request? Or did they communicate, in effect, "Do it because I say so"?

4. Did you feel free to express your views openly, without fear of punishment?

5. Did your parents communicate their disapproval of your thoughts, desires or behavior by means of humor, teasing or sarcasm?

6. Did your parents treat you with respect?

Supplementary questions:

Were your thoughts, needs, and feelings given consideration?

Was your dignity as a human being acknowledged?

When you expressed ideas or opinions, were they treated seriously?

Were your likes and dislikes treated seriously?

(Not necessarily agreed with or acceded to, but nonetheless treated seriously?)

Were your desires treated thoughtfully and respectfully?

7. Did you feel that you were psychologically visible to your parents? Did you feel real to them?

   Supplementary questions:
   Did your parents seem to make a genuine, thoughtful effort to understand you?
   Did your parents seem authentically interested in you as a person?
   Could you talk to your parents about issues of importance and receive interested, meaningful understanding from them?

8. Did you feel loved and valued by your parents, in the sense that you experienced yourself as a source of pleasure to them? Or did you feel unwanted, perhaps a burden? Or did you feel hated? Or did you feel you were simply an object of indifference?

9. Did your parents deal with you fairly and justly?

   Supplementary questions:
   Did your parents resort to threats in order to control your behavior—either threats of immediate punitive action on their part, or threats in terms of long-range consequences for your life, or threats of supernatural punishments, such as going to hell?
   Were you praised when you performed well? or merely criticized when you performed badly?
   Were your parents willing to admit it when they were wrong? Or was it against their policy to concede that they were wrong?

10. Was it your parents' practice to punish you or discipline you by striking or beating you?

11. Did your parents project that they believed in your basic goodness? Or did they project that they saw you as bad or worthless or evil?

12. Did your parents project that they believed in your intellectual and creative potentialities? Or did they project that they saw you as mediocre or stupid or inadequate?

13. In your parents' expectations concerning your behavior and performance, did they take cognizance of your knowledge, needs, interests and context? Or were you confronted by expectations and demands that were overwhelming and beyond your ability to satisfy?

14. Did your parents' behavior and manner of dealing with you tend to produce guilt in you?

15. Did your parents' behavior and manner of dealing with you tend to produce fear in you?

16. Did your parents respect your intellectual and physical privacy?

17. Did your parents project that it was desirable for you to think well of yourself, to have self-esteem? Or were you cautioned against valuing yourself, and encouraged to be humble?

18. Did your parents project that what a person made of his life, and what you specifically made of your life, was important?

Supplementary questions:

Did your parents project that great things are possible to human beings—and specifically, great things are possible to you?

Did your parents project that life could be

an exciting, challenging and rewarding adventure?

19. Did your parents encourage in you a fear of the world, a fear of other people? Or were you encouraged to face the world with an attitude of relaxed, confident benevolence? Or neither?

20. Were you encouraged to be open in the expression of your emotions and desires? Or were your parents' behavior and manner of treating you such as to make you fear emotional self-assertiveness and openness, or to regard it as inappropriate?

21. Did your parents encourage you in the direction of having a healthy, affirmative attitude toward sex and toward your own body? Or a negative attitude? Or neither?

22. Did your parents' manner of dealing with you tend to develop and strengthen your sense of your masculinity or femininity? Or to frustrate and diminish it? Or neither?

During the weeks and months following the formulation of these questions, I used them with eighty or ninety clients in group or individual therapy.

The material in succeeding chapters is taken from *initial* discussions with clients concerning one or another of these questions; I do not include follow-up sessions, since that is not essential to my purpose here, which is to clarify the significance of these questions and to indicate the way in which they can be used therapeutically.

The Unknowable

When you were a child, did your parents' manner of behaving and of dealing with you give you the impression that you were living in a world that was rational, predictable, intelligible? Or a world that was bewildering, contradictory, incomprehensible, unknowable?

Client: Henry, twenty-four years old.

BRANDEN: Henry, let me begin by explaining what I'm after in this question and why the issue is important.

One of the most valuable things that parents can do to encourage the healthy development of a child's mind is to create a rational, stable and predictable home environment, so that the child feels his mind is capable of understanding the world around him. If the child is made to feel that he's caught in an unpredictable, unintelligible world—and, therefore, a frightening world—the danger is that he will surrender his will to

16

understand, give up in despair, and conclude that there's no point in trying to think, since his thinking can avail him nothing, since the world is not to be understood, not by him, not by his mind.

To give you a more detailed picture of what this issue involves, I'd like to read something to you. Perhaps you'll remember it; it's from *The Psychology of Self-Esteem,* where I describe the kind of irrational home atmosphere so many children are brought up in:

"In the case of the man we are considering, the irrationality to which he was exposed as a child was not the expression of intentional cruelty or ill will. It was simply the 'normal' manner of functioning, on the part of his parents, which most adults take for granted.

"It consisted of such things as: making promises capriciously and breaking them capriciously— over-solicitude when the parent was in one mood, and callous remoteness when the parent was in another—answering questions pleasantly one day, and irritably dismissing them the next— sudden explosions of love followed by sudden explosions of resentment—arbitrary, unexplained rules and arbitrary, unexplained exceptions— unexpected rewards and unprovoked punishments—subtle pressures, gentle sarcasms, smiling lies, masquerading as affection and parental devotion—switching, irreconcilable commandments—vagueness and ambiguity and impatience and coldness and hysteria and indulgence and reproaches and anxious tenderness."

HENRY: Perhaps we should try another question. I'm drawing a blank on this.

BRANDEN: No, let's stay with it.... What are you feeling right now?

HENRY: I don't know. All of a sudden, I feel sleepy. I've had enough sleep. I don't know what's the matter with me.

BRANDEN: Sometimes, when people are up against issues they don't want to face, especially things that are painful and that they feel powerless to change, they become exhausted; it hits them suddenly, out of nowhere—a sense of immense weight, as if it's too much of an effort even to keep their eyes open. . . . So start talking.

HENRY: My father didn't create the sense of a contradictory world. He was consistent—perversely consistent. He always gave me the impression that I was an imposition on him. And a disappointment.

BRANDEN: Did he ever indicate why?

HENRY: It was his whole attitude. He never explained anything. He just got the message across—nothing I could do was right. It was always on his face. From the day I was born. Impatience. Irritation. Contempt.

BRANDEN: And did that make sense to you? Did it seem fair?

HENRY: No. I didn't see why I should get treated that way. Oh, is that what you mean by the sense of a crazy world?

BRANDEN: That's part of it. What else did your father do?

HENRY: He would sit for hours, sometimes, not talking, not doing anything. You wouldn't dare speak to him or ask him anything. If I made the slightest noise, the roof would fall in on me. How can you not make noise when you're four or five years old?

BRANDEN: What about your mother? What did she project?

HENRY: My mother is okay. She's very nervous. She never seemed to know what to do with me. She had her own troubles.

BRANDEN: Such as?

HENRY: She was always crying about something. She would talk to me about it. I never knew what she was talking about. I was three years old when she began making me her marriage counselor.

BRANDEN: Are you able to say what you felt for your father when you were a little boy?

HENRY: I loved him, I suppose.

BRANDEN: Imagine you're in the house and your father hasn't come home yet. Now you hear his footsteps. He's coming home. What do you feel?

HENRY: What kind of a mood will he be in? I hope he'll be cheerful. Sometimes he is. Sometimes he's in a bad mood and he yells at me. I feel fear. I never know what to expect. I never know what will make him angry. I don't know why he has to yell so much. ... Oh, Christ ...

BRANDEN: That's all right. There's nothing wrong with crying. ... It must be very hard, being a little boy in that kind of home.

HENRY: My mother is always talking about heaven. How we'll all be happy when we go to heaven. What has that got to do with anything? Do you know what I mean?

BRANDEN: Spell it out.

HENRY: It's like ... everything Mother says is irrelevant ... and most of what Father says is frightening. So where are you?
I was playing with some matches once. I set some leaves on fire in the backyard. Father said the police would come and take me away. He said they would take me to Juvenile Hall. Then Mother came and put her arms around me and told me I was her darling angel. Then Father began yelling. I think he got mad at her and forgot all about me. I remember, later that evening, he gave me a present. I never understood it. He was smiling and cheerful like what happened earlier had never happened.
But I couldn't stand all the shouting in the house. There was always shouting, and my mother was always afraid, always crying and talking about heaven and Jesus and hugging me and looking off into space and not even knowing she was holding me.

BRANDEN: You must have felt terribly frustrated.

HENRY: Frustrated, yes. And afraid. I felt afraid of people. I've always been very shy.

BRANDEN: Do you remember feeling helpless very often?

HENRY: No.

BRANDEN: What was that long pause and that funny look all about?

HENRY: I don't know. I guess I'm surprised that I didn't feel helpless. That's all. I just felt terror.

BRANDEN: You felt terror but you didn't feel helplessness?

HENRY: Well, maybe I did feel some helplessness. I'd just turn them off. Then I'd feel better.

BRANDEN: Turn them off?

HENRY: Yeah. Make them go away. Like they didn't exist. Like it wasn't happening to me. It's hard to explain.

BRANDEN: You didn't want to feel helpless. I wonder what happened to all the other emotions you must have felt—frustration, bewilderment, hurt, anger, rage.

HENRY: Oh, I never felt rage!

BRANDEN: No?

HENRY: If I had felt rage, my father would have killed me!

BRANDEN: Come on now. That may have been a reason not to show him your rage. But would that
have stopped you from feeling it?

HENRY: I turned them both off—both my parents—so
I wouldn't have to feel it.

BRANDEN: There are other emotions besides rage that
you didn't want to feel, weren't there?

HENRY: I don't remember.

BRANDEN: Yes, you do.

HENRY: I wanted to feel in control.

BRANDEN: So you repressed every emotion that threatened your control. You wanted the sense that you
were secure, that everything was all right, that
there was nothing to be afraid of—and so you
denied and blocked off any threatening feelings,
anything that would throw off your equilibrium,
or your pretense at it.

HENRY: Well, what was I supposed to do?

BRANDEN: Did you know, at the time, what you were
doing?

HENRY: I don't think I knew any of this at the
time. . . .
I mean, what was the point of trying to understand them? It was impossible.
That passage you read from your book—brother,
that was written about me!

BRANDEN: I felt it was about you, when I was reading.
It was on your face.

HENRY: What?

TED (another client): I was watching him while you were reading. He wasn't showing anything.

BRANDEN: He was trying too hard not to show anything. Henry, what are you feeling now?

HENRY: Anger. And relief.

TED: Could he have helped himself at the time? Did he have to withdraw?

BRANDEN: What do you think, Henry?

HENRY: It felt like the only solution.

BRANDEN: When you withdrew, you gave up the hope of understanding. You stopped caring to understand. That's when you gave up your self-esteem.

HENRY: When I turned inward, I think I turned myself off, too, I turned off something inside me.

BRANDEN: That's what we have to turn on again.
Do you remember what you said your problem was, that first day you came to see me? You said you felt cut off from the world, you had no ambition, you didn't want anything. Are you beginning to understand how it happened? Part of how it happened? Because there's more to it than this, of course. This is just one aspect. But it's an important aspect.

HENRY: Oh, yes. Most of this, I had no idea of. I never even thought about my parents. They're still living, but two thousand miles away, so I never have to see them. They want to know why I never write letters. I'd like to kill that son of a bitch!

BRANDEN: It's good that you know it.
You don't have to be afraid that you'll act on it. But it's important for you to know what you feel.

HENRY: I always felt that there must be something wrong with me. There had to be. I couldn't understand. I couldn't believe parents would treat you that way, for no reason whatever.

BRANDEN: You took the blame. That's how they got you. You knew there was a fault somewhere and you assumed it was yours. Perhaps that seemed easier—less frightening than the alternative. But when you gave up the effort to think and judge. . . .

HENRY: They got me, all right.

BRANDEN: It can be very difficult when you're young. You don't have the knowledge to understand how irrational your parents are being. You don't know how to interpret their behavior. It's not always possible to be sure of your own judgment. But as you grew older, when more knowledge was available to you, how hard did you try to think things out then, I wonder, how hard did you try to understand the situation?

HENRY: I didn't try at all. I just withdrew.

BRANDEN: That's where you did yourself damage. And are still doing yourself damage—every time you surrender to fear, every time you withdraw and turn off your mind, every time you retreat into dreams when you're in a situation requiring that you think.

Could you have avoided withdrawing and repressing, when you were young? Yes, probably you could have done better than you did. But to hell with that. The question is: what are you going to do now? Because you can certainly do better now.

MARY (another client): Why didn't he come out of his shell when he grew older?

BRANDEN: As you've heard him say, he didn't think about it, then or later. He remained passive. He turned his mind off and left it off. Project what would have happened to him as he grew older. He was not concerned to understand the world around him. He wasn't concerned with his own intellectual growth and development. He wasn't concerned to learn the things that are a normal part of growing up. So, very often, when he tried to act, his ignorance would make him ineffectual; he would fail in what he was doing. Isn't that right, Henry?

HENRY: Absolutely.

BRANDEN: And the repeated failures would only reinforce his initial premise: that he is helpless, that the world is not for him to understand, that there is something wrong with him—that life on earth is impossible for him. So a vicious circle is set up. If he understands it, perhaps he'll choose to break out of it.

MARY: Will he feel this anger against his parents permanently?

BRANDEN: No. But I want him to feel it now. I want
him to feel it all—fully. Those feelings contain
the story of how he perceived the world then,
how he perceived the situation he was caught in
and what it meant to him. So we have to get it
all out. Then we can untangle it. We can learn
what conclusions he drew from those early experiences. Some of those conclusions are already
obvious.

Then Henry, when you're free of it all, when
you've thrown off all the harmful effects, you'll
be free of the anger, too. It won't matter anymore.
It won't be part of your present life. You'll have
reclaimed your self-esteem.

All right, that's enough for now. We'll talk about
this more another time. Henry, I want you to do a
written assignment. Do a paper summarizing
what you've understood from today's discussion.
Perhaps you'll want to relate other incidents in
your childhood that encouraged the belief that
you were helpless to understand the world
around you, or that otherwise contributed to your
negative self-concept. See what else you can
identify.

Right now, let's move on to another person and
work with a different question.

The Surrender

Were you taught the importance of learning to think, the importance of developing your mind, the importance of becoming a rational being? Did your parents provide you with intellectual stimulation and convey the idea that the use of your mind can be an exciting pleasure?

Client: Alfred, twenty-two years old.

BRANDEN: The primary task of parenthood is to equip a child for independent survival as an adult. That entails doing everything in the parent's power to encourage the child's development as a rational, thinking being.

Alfred, how did your parents handle this matter? What's your immediate reaction to my question?

ALFRED: Are you kidding? I was born Catholic.

BRANDEN: What does that mean?

ALFRED: It means I had a real groovy childhood.

BRANDEN: Did you experience it as enjoyable or funny at the time?

ALFRED: It was murder.

BRANDEN: Do you make it less murderous by joking about it now?

ALFRED: Either I joke or I scream.

BRANDEN: Then scream. That takes more courage. And it's more useful.

ALFRED: I remember my mother helping my brothers and sisters do their homework. If they didn't see something, she practically would beat it into them. She really knew how to swear.

BRANDEN: Is that how she treated you?

ALFRED: She never had to. School was always easy for me. So I suppose you would have to say that Mother was interested in the development of our minds. My father was sort of indifferent. But Mother was very concerned that we do our duties: school work, helping with the dishes, that kind of thing.

BRANDEN: Almost all parents want their children to do well in school. That has virtually nothing to do with wanting their children to develop into thinking beings—at least, not necessarily.

If learning is treated as a duty, as a painful obligation, as something you have to do to keep your parents happy or to keep them from yelling at you, that's not teaching children the value of rationality. That's not teaching them to love the power of their own minds.

DONALD (another client): Suppose parents did want to teach a child to be rational and to develop his thinking ability. What would they do?

BRANDEN: Okay, let's pause on that.

It's not an issue simply of what the parents might tell the child, but of the parents' total behavior and way of functioning. Parents' most potent tool of teaching is through example. Hysterically irrational parents are never going to inspire their child to be rational, regardless of what kind of lectures they might deliver to him on the subject of rationality.

There are many things a parent can do. First, there is the matter of giving a child the sense of living in a rational world which his mind is able to understand. We've already talked about that.

Then, the parents can help by providing the child with adequate stimulation: sensory stimulation, when the child is an infant, permitting and encouraging him to explore his physical environment and to use all of his senses, providing him with many objects of different colors, sizes and shapes that he can look at, taste, touch, feel, and so forth; then, when the child is a little older, providing him with conceptual stimulation, encouraging his curiosity, answering his questions with interest and enthusiasm, introducing him to books, inviting his participation in serious discussions, and so forth.

As the child is developing his ability to think, parents should try to make him conscious of his own mental processes—make him aware that he is thinking, make him proud of it, emphasize the virtue and value of it. But in a relaxed, nonpedantic way—don't make it a lecture.

Communicate the excitement of learning, the excitement of acquiring knowledge, the excitement of meeting new challenges to one's mind. Communicate confidence in the child's ability to understand, to master difficult problems. Never, never insult the child's mind if he doesn't understand something; never disparage his mental capacity by calling him stupid. What if he believes and accepts your insults? Then what happens to him?

Teach the child to be aware of the distinction between a thought and an emotion; and not to treat thinking and feeling as interchangeable functions. Teach him that emotions are not tools of knowledge. Teach him the importance of being guided by reason in his actions.

Do not encourage a child in the belief that the irrational can succeed—that by pouting or crying or "acting cute" he can get something which he should not have, which is bad for him, or to which he is not entitled. This is what it really means to "spoil" a child; it's not a matter of giving him too many toys or too much affection, but of indulging him in the belief that reality, and the parents' judgment of reality, can be subordinated to his feelings and desires. That's the kind of mistake "loving" parents make every day, and it's disastrous.

There's much more to be said on this subject. These are just a few major points. But it's enough to give you a general indication of the direction parents should follow.

ALFRED: What we were taught mostly was the virtue of humility. It's better to walk with your eyes looking down. Don't ask questions. Don't argue with your elders. Be super-respectful with the priest. Stand up when your elders come into the room. Or else you'll burn in hell.

BRANDEN: Go on.

ALFRED: You're bad anyway, so don't make it worse— by thinking you're too smart. That kind of thing. Also, don't play with yourself. Whatever else you do, don't play with yourself. It doesn't matter if you're the stupidest moron who ever lived, but just don't play with yourself; keep yourself pure, and you'll be all right.

BRANDEN: In other words, your body—and sexual pleasure—are evil.

ALFRED: "Evil" doesn't say the half of it. My mother could think of more ways to get the idea across that sex is dirty and foul and rotten than anybody I've ever heard of. My father wouldn't say that much, just a warning now and then; but he'd always look at me as though he were searching for evidence of some sexual perversion. The nuns at school had some things to say, too, of course. . . .
The idea of God used to bother me a lot.

BRANDEN: In what way?

ALFRED: I don't know, it just made everything shaky. Like the world would never come into focus for me. It was frightening. He was so . . . unsolid . . . yet He was supposed to be more important than

anything else. It was frightening, and I felt guilty
because it was frightening. Instead of feeling
love, I felt fear. That showed disrespect.... I
didn't like the idea that God could see everything a person did, like someone always spying
on you. I felt I had a right to privacy. Then I felt
guilty over that, too. Boy, this is painful!

BRANDEN: Talk about what you're feeling right now.

ALFRED: Let me tell you.... Once I asked our priest
something about God, some question, I forget
what it was.... Oh, I don't know, something
like: where did God live before He created the
universe? ... The priest got red in the face. I felt
sure he was going to start swearing at me.

BRANDEN: All right, close your eyes, take a deep breath
and relax. You're talking to the priest right now.
You're looking up at him. He's angry. What are
you feeling?

ALFRED: Like he's out to get me—no, not just him, but
something else, something immense is out to get
me, to hurt me or crush me or....

BRANDEN: What have you done wrong? What sin have
you committed?

ALFRED: Just the sin of being me, I guess. Like it was
a sin to see too much, a sin to lift your eyes off
the ground....

BRANDEN: Did you feel it was a sin?

ALFRED: I felt there was something wrong with me.
And I hated everybody for it. And I felt guilty
over that.

BRANDEN: Isn't it part of their teachings that there is "something wrong" with you by your very nature? Isn't that entailed in the concept of Original Sin?

ALFRED: That's right.

BRANDEN: As for your hating everybody else, I wonder if you felt that way because you saw them as being, in effect, part of a conspiracy, in that they were going along with or sanctioning or voicing on their own the things you were being taught, the things you felt were destroying you.

ALFRED: How in hell did you know that?

BRANDEN: I've been listening to you.

ALFRED: I felt that my sin . . . my sin was that I didn't believe in Original Sin. It's such bullshit.

BRANDEN: I know that. But do you know it?

ALFRED: Oh, I'm through with all that crap. That's not my problem.

PHILIP (another client): What's your problem?

ALFRED: Anxiety. Depression. Screwing around too much. Almost getting thrown out of school for low grades. Did I tell you that I was in a genius category on the IQ test?

BRANDEN: What does that mean to you? What does that fact make you feel?

ALFRED: It doesn't mean anything. So what?

BRANDEN: What did you want to scream about?

ALFRED: Huh?

BRANDEN: You said you'd have to either joke or scream. Scream about what?

ALFRED: That was a figure of speech. What I really want is to forget all about them—my mother and father and the whole goddamn family and the priest and everybody else I knew when I was growing up. Do we have to talk about this? ... You know something? *They didn't want me to be intelligent.* What do you think of that?

BRANDEN: When did you come to that conclusion?

ALFRED: Just now.

BRANDEN: Alfred, think about this. What's your estimate of people who resent intelligence? What's your estimate of people who resent a boy that asks questions? Who wants to understand things? who won't accept things blindly on faith? What's your estimate of people who want to crush you because you can think? Who want to make you feel guilty because you can think?

ALFRED: I'd like to get some whore and screw her in church.

BRANDEN: What could that do for you?

ALFRED: I don't know. It would be a nice gesture. Emotionally satisfying.

BRANDEN: Do you think that's why you handle your sex life as you do? As an act of defiance?

ALFRED: Hey—probably. That's good.

BRANDEN: Do you get pleasure out of it?

ALFRED: I don't get pleasure out of anything. That's one of the reasons I'm here.

BRANDEN: Alfred, don't you see? You've made them your masters—your mother and father, the priest, everybody who hurt you. Everybody you have to defy. You're a puppet and they're pulling the strings. Only it's in reverse. Instead of doing everything they want you to do, you do everything they don't want you to do. But it's still those people who are controlling you. It isn't your desires that motivate you—it's theirs. Theirs, turned backwards. They tell you you're evil, so to defy them, you do things that cause you to despise yourself. And so you fall into their trap. Who wins? Who defeats whom?

ALFRED: I feel like I'm going to explode. I feel like there's garbage inside me I want to vomit up.

BRANDEN: There is garbage inside you. All the poison you've permitted yourself to absorb from them. All the unwarranted guilt. It's going to take courage—for you to admit the amount of that poison you're still carrying. It's going to take strength and patience to work through all of it, and get rid of it, once and for all.

You'd like to be free of them—really free of them —free of everything you've absorbed that's still choking you: you'd like to be your own man. You'd like to be a different kind of human being than you've ever been.

ALFRED: Yes.

BRANDEN: Well, you can be. There's nothing to stop you. You know that, don't you?

ALFRED: Right now, I know it.

BRANDEN: Then it's this moment that you'll have to remember, the way things look to you right now—that's what you'll have to call on and remind yourself of when you're alone and you're feeling like hell.

JEFF (another client): I can really identify with this. Most of the things you're talking about are directly applicable to me; in fact, I can't think what isn't applicable.
I understand what he means by God making the world seem shaky. It's—it's supernatural, and so it dissolves your sense of the reality of anything ... Didn't you talk about that once, in one of your lectures?

BRANDEN: Yes.

JEFF: We accept so many of the things our parents and the church teach us—but then, on a higher level of our mind, we repudiate it, and then rebel against it. But, why doesn't the repudiation go all the way down?

ALFRED: I think I know, damn it. It's because the repudiation is not really thought out, it's just emotional. It's just a feeling they're wrong.

MARY (another client): And that's not good enough. You have to have knowledge.

BRANDEN: You have to have rational conviction.

JEFF: But hell—I'm rationally convinced today.

ALFRED: Yes, but don't you see? It's what N.B. was saying. You felt guilty because you were not really that certain. But you wanted to defy them. So you do stupid, irrational things—things that would make anyone feel guilt. I mean real guilt, rational guilt. Then your own sense of guilt and unworthiness works against you, undermines you, disarms you, makes you feel: Christ, I am a sinner, they were right, I'm no good, I'm contaminated, I'm unclean, I can't set myself against them, I can't fight them, I'm out of the race, I'm disqualified. . . . That's the trap, isn't it?

BRANDEN: That's the trap. Very good. And you're being serious.

ALFRED: I feel shy.

BRANDEN: That won't kill you.

The Pressure Chamber

Were you encouraged to think independently, to develop your critical faculty? Or were you taught to be obedient rather than mentally active and questioning.

Did your parents project that it was more important to conform to what other people believed than to discover what is true?

When your parents wanted you to do something, did they appeal to your understanding and give you reasons for their request? Or did they communicate, in effect, "Do it because I say so"?

Client: Martha, nineteen years old.

BRANDEN: Martha, I'm giving you these three questions, rather than a single question, to indicate the general territory I want to get into right now. You can respond to any of the questions you wish, or all three of them.

MARTHA: This is difficult. I don't feel that any of the alternatives quite fit me. I don't know how you would describe what happened.

I was ordered to be independent. I was threatened and yelled at: I absolutely must be independent.

This was my mother's position. My father stayed out of it; he stayed out of everything, as though he had no opinions about me or anything else. He was just there, but he never said anything.

BRANDEN: What did your mother seem to mean by "being independent"?

MARTHA: I must never hesitate, I must never make a mistake, I must never be confused, I must always know what to do. I must always know right now, immediately, the second anything arises. No time to wonder or to be in doubt.

BRANDEN: Give an example.

MARTHA: Mother would give me some household chore to do, but she wouldn't explain specifically what she wanted done, so perhaps I wouldn't know how to carry it out. Then, when I'd look puzzled or confused, she'd tell me I wasn't doing my own thinking, wasn't being independent. Everything was supposed to be self-evident, I guess.

BRANDEN: Could you give another example?

MARTHA: When Mother would talk to my teachers at school, they would tell her I was terrible— rebellious and disobedient. It would upset her. She took it as a personal disgrace to her and got very angry at me. There would be this contradiction: she would tell me I was stupid—and that with my brains I should be at the top of the class.

It's getting clearer now.... Mother cared very much what everyone thought of her and of me, but she wouldn't admit it. I think she's a very hostile person. It was very important to her that I do well—so that she could show me off. I was her claim to fame. And I felt that if my performance didn't suit her, I was threatening to her and she hated me.

BRANDEN: Is that teaching you to be independent? Is that teaching you that your life belongs to you, that you must be free to learn, to grow and to make your own mistakes?

MARTHA: I wasn't permitted mistakes. I wasn't given much freedom either; I always had to give an exact account of what I was doing, or where I'd been, or even, sometimes, what I was thinking about. I don't know what she was afraid I might do, but she sure was afraid of something.

BRANDEN: What did that make you feel?

MARTHA: Different things at different times. There must be something wrong with me. I must be bad in some way that Mother is able to see. Also, it made me furious with anger—because I didn't see what I was doing that was bad. It seemed so unfair.

BRANDEN: From the perspective of today, do you think your mother really understood the meaning of independence? Or that she really wanted you to be independent?

MARTHA: Of course not. I see that now. I wish I'd known it then.

BRANDEN: Many different elements go into encouraging a child to become independent. One, of course, is teaching him the importance of thinking. Another is teaching him that *what he thinks is important.* Do you see that those are two different issues?

MARTHA: Oh, yes!

BRANDEN: I want you to understand this, so let's consider it further.

If parents want to see their child grow up to be independent, it's important that they communicate respect for the child's mind, respect for the child's efforts to understand, respect for the child's thinking processes. Perhaps the real test for the parents comes when the child makes a mistake, makes an error of judgment. It's easy enough to applaud a child when he's right—although most parents don't do that, either. But when his judgment is wrong and they must correct him, it's then that their skill as parents is challenged.

One can correct a child in a way that tends to crush his efforts at independent thought, one can correct him in a way that communicates contempt. Or one can correct him in a relaxed manner, be interested in why he came to the conclusion he did, be patient and sympathetic in pointing out his error, be more concerned to support and develop his intellectual self-confidence than to hammer the right answer down his throat.

Very few parents know how to correct a child properly. They're too concerned with the child having what they, the parents, believe to be the right answers. They don't care enough about how he gets them. But *how* he arrives at his conclusions is more important than whether any particular conclusion is correct or mistaken.

MARTHA: If it's a crime to make a mistake, how can you be independent? How can you venture forth and try things on your own? If you know someone is just waiting, ready to leap on you? It's too frightening.

KEITH (another client): Martha's mother reminds me of my father. This is really illuminating for me. If I do anything wrong, he absolutely takes it as a disgrace to himself, as a reflection on his worth as a parent. I never thought about it that way before. But that's what his anger is all about. If I make a mistake, he's threatened.

MARTHA: Mother was always very suspicious, as if she expected the worst of me—and probably of everyone else—and she was waiting in trembling anxiety for her child's deficiency or depravity to reveal itself. . . .

BRANDEN: That would have had to strengthen your fear that there was something wrong with you— or else just totally bewilder you—or both.

MARTHA: You know, I always took pride in the fact that I never hit her; I never struck back or yelled, even when she hit me or screamed at me. That was very important to me.

BRANDEN: Elaborate on that.

MARTHA: I don't know what to say.

BRANDEN: Close your eyes. Take a long, slow, deep breath and let yourself relax. You're seven years old. Your mother is hitting you and screaming at you. What do you feel?

MARTHA: You can hurt me if you want to; I love you.

BRANDEN: Go on.

MARTHA: That's all.

BRANDEN: What if you don't love her? What if you hate her?

MARTHA: She'll kill me.

BRANDEN: What will you do with the rage you feel?

MARTHA: I mustn't feel rage. Why doesn't my father say anything? Why doesn't he do anything? Why does he just stand by and let it happen?

BRANDEN: You feel abandoned.

MARTHA: Betrayed. I don't trust anyone. I'm suspicious when people are nice to me.

BRANDEN: What are you feeling right now?

MARTHA: Frustrated rage. All that time I wanted to kill her. Now I can say it. I'd like to scream it. . . . All through my life I was afraid my mother might be right.

BRANDEN: That you really are a bad person?

MARTHA: That I'll never succeed in anything. That
  I'll never know what to do. How can you tell a
  child to be independent and then say that children should be seen and not heard? Mother was
  only half kidding when she'd say that. She meant
  it. She didn't want me to be heard—unless someone was in the house she wanted to impress. I
  felt used; I always felt used.
  If I solve my problems and make something of
  my life, do you know what Mother will say? "I
  always said you could. You see, I was right."
  I'm feeling better now. It doesn't seem so painful.

BRANDEN: You just thought of something. What is it?

MARTHA: If you're always trying to guess what somebody expects of you, what somebody expects you
  to think or do, how do you ever get in touch
  with reality? I mean, the real world?

BRANDEN: Exactly. Why did that occur to you now?

MARTHA: I feel as though all my life I've been struggling ... to get to reality ... to get my own mind
  working ... and Mother was like a big wall,
  always in the way. She's very intelligent; she
  really is.

BRANDEN: That would make you more vulnerable to
  her, wouldn't it? If many of the things she told
  you made sense, really made sense to you—if she
  gave you reason to respect her judgment—
  couldn't that tend to disarm you when she was

being irrational? You'd be much more inclined to
give her the benefit of the doubt—at your own
expense.

MARTHA: Yes.

BRANDEN: Is all this coming into clearer perspective?

MARTHA: I want to go home and write a paper on
this. I think a lot of my hostility is tied up with
what we're talking about. Don't you?

BRANDEN: Yes.

MARTHA: I want to think about that. I have an idea
when I hand you the paper it's going to be
soaking wet. Know what I mean?

BRANDEN: I'm not afraid of tears. I can take it.

MARTHA: Well, I guess I can take it, too—I hope.

The Inheritance

Did you feel free to express your views openly, without fear of punishment?

Client: Helen, twenty-eight years old.

BRANDEN: How would you answer that question, Helen?

HELEN: Oh, God, I feel guilty already.

BRANDEN: Why?

HELEN: Because I don't think I act right as a parent, myself. Sometimes, when my son, Tony, expresses ideas I think are ridiculous, I really let him have it. So does his father. I guess we're both making a mistake. It just gets so exasperating at times, though.

BRANDEN: Tell me about it.

HELEN: Sometimes Tony comes home from school and he starts attacking his teacher. I've met his teacher and she's a perfectly lovely woman. For some reason she seems to antagonize Tony or he seems to antagonize her; anyway, he's always insisting she's dumb. It makes me furious; it seems so unfair. So I lose my temper and start shouting at him.

Another thing. He brings those ridiculous comic books into the house. Once I said something about one of them, and he began to argue with me. I don't know what came over me—I just swung out and slapped him. I felt terrible afterward, because he wasn't being unreasonable or bad tempered or anything. But I get these explosions now and again. Sometimes he really is disrespectful, but sometimes it's just my imagination—which I don't realize until it's too late.

I'm afraid my husband is a worse offender. Tony is getting so he's afraid to say anything when Daddy is around.

BRANDEN: Let's get back to your own childhood. How did your parents treat you?

HELEN: My parents had a very strong sense of—what would you call it?—a family hierarchy. The hierarchy of command or rank. My father was the absolute authority in the house. His word was law; no one dared challenge or question him about anything. Then came Mother. Her rank was less; she would always defer to Father. But it was pretty dangerous for us to disagree with her. We could get away with it occasionally, but not often. We kids—there were five of us—had no position whatsoever. It was sort of political: we were the subjects, Mother and Father were the ruling class.

BRANDEN: Were you never permitted to express a disagreement with your parents? Or to challenge them about anything?

HELEN: Only if we were willing to risk punishment.

BRANDEN: Give an example.

HELEN: It's hard to remember. Well, let's see. . . . Here's something. This is going to sound silly but . . . we were having a party. Mother wanted me to wear one dress; I wanted to wear a different one. The result was I stayed in my room and was not permitted to come down to the party. I'd committed the sin of arguing with Mother.

BRANDEN: One more example.

HELEN: Father had a cousin who visited us occasionally. But Father disliked him. Once I said I liked Jack—that was his name—and Father said that he didn't want me to spend too much time in the living room when Jack was there. I asked why. Father just froze and looked at me and said, "Because I told you."
You should have asked me that question about independence. That's all we ever heard— "Because I say so." Their theory, I guess, was that thinking is a privilege of adulthood.

BRANDEN: It's a privilege I wish they'd chosen to exercise. . . . What did their way of doing things make you feel?

HELEN: I've been thinking about that, Nathan. I mean, during the past hour or so, while some of the others have been talking. If they hadn't spoken

first, I don't think I'd have the courage to say
this. I'm not sure I'd even be aware of it.
It really hurt me. And frightened me. I was
frightened all the time. All through growing up.
It was like living in a dictatorship. Oh, God, it
was awful! It made me feel so helpless! I was
just ... just nothing! They could do anything
they wanted and I had no rights. I wasn't a
human being; I was an object. I was their possession.

BRANDEN: When you were young and all this was
happening, you must have felt many painful
emotions: fear, bewilderment, anger, rage, indig-
nation.

HELEN: It's hard to remember now. My feeling is that I
repressed all that. Because if anybody had stopped
me on the street yesterday and asked me, I would
have sworn I had a lovely childhood.

BRANDEN: What happened to all those emotions you
never faced, never dealt with—all that pain you
never resolved, all that hurt and rage that's still
there, inside you?

HELEN: I don't know.

BRANDEN: Yes, you do. You've already told us.
You stored it all up. You saved it. As an inheritance—to pass on to your son.

The Barbarians

Did your parents communicate their disapproval of your thoughts, desires or behavior by means of humor, teasing or sarcasm?

Client: Robert, eighteen years old.

BRANDEN: What do you say, Robert?

ROBERT: Don't you think humor can sometimes be appropriate?

BRANDEN: That depends.

ROBERT: I mean, some things are funny, N.B. When you're young, you often do funny things.

BRANDEN: Like what?

ROBERT: Oh, I don't know . . . well, like maybe, let me see . . . it's hard to think of an example.

BRANDEN: Stop stalling.

ROBERT: Like playing Batman or—

BRANDEN: What's funny about that?

ROBERT: You don't think it's funny?

BRANDEN: No. I did that when I was a boy. It was serious to me. Wasn't it serious to you?

ROBERT: Yeah, but that's what's funny.

BRANDEN: Do you really think so? Well, go ahead. What about teasing and sarcasm?

ROBERT: My parents like to kid a lot. Which is sort of weird, because they've both got tempers, too. One moment they're being funny, and the next moment they're hitting you on the head and telling you you're a rotten pig.

BRANDEN: Those two characteristics often go together. Give me some examples of their sarcasm.

ROBERT: That's hard to do, because their attitude goes through everything; it's in their whole manner. It's just their outlook, their outlook on life. When I was young, I used to eat too fast—as a matter of fact I still do—and Father might say, with a big grin on his face and a real bite in his voice, "Are you trying to see if you can make me vomit from just looking at you?" Let's see. . . . Oh yeah, I'd have a girlfriend over to the house and Mother might say, "Can I talk to you a minute, Flash Gordon?" Or I'd be listening to music by myself, and I'd be conducting—you know, wav-

ing my arms and all—and Mother would come
into the room, unexpectedly. I wouldn't hear her,
and she'd smirk and say: "Toscanini, do you
think you could condescend to help your sister
with her homework?" If I liked a certain movie
actor, I wouldn't dare mention it, because if I
did, my father would really go to work on him
with the needle—you know, really tear him
apart, as though what kind of a jerk was I to like
such a person, he was probably a fag or. . . .
Why couldn't they just talk to me normally? Why
. . . oh, shit. . . .

BRANDEN: It's stopped being funny.

ROBERT: It really hurt, you know. I mean, all the time
—they were at it all the time.

BRANDEN: I understand.

ROBERT: Mother thinks she's the greatest mother on
earth. She sees herself as a great pal to me. She's
very informal. I wouldn't object to some formali-
ty. Why should people talk to each other that
way?

BRANDEN: What are you feeling?

ROBERT: Hurt. Really hurt. Really, really hurt.

BRANDEN: The other day a woman came to see me
with her thirteen-year-old daughter. She wanted
me to work with the daughter, because her
daughter, she said, threw screaming fits. I asked
the mother why she thought her daughter did it.
She looked at me as if she thought it were an
irrelevant question—obviously one she never

thought to ask herself, or to ask her daughter. So I asked the girl, right there. The girl began to cry, and answered: "Because they're always teasing me and making fun of me and criticizing me, and they'll never listen to me about anything." Whereupon the mother said, "Listen to her? Of course we listen to her. You should hear the kind of things she says. She's so immature. She told me she sees herself as a wild stallion that no one can tame. All I did was try to explain to her why it's foolish for a thirteen-year-old girl to call herself a stallion, and she began to scream." Then the mother began to laugh, as though it were a joke she was sharing with me, looking at me for sympathy and support. I don't mind admitting I wanted to slap her face.

ROBERT: What did you do?

BRANDEN: I explained to her what her daughter was really saying, and why it was normal and valid for her to think in terms of a metaphor, such as a wild stallion, with whom she identified. The girl was trying to say that she was determined not to let her parents break her spirit, no matter what they did. It was obvious. The mother looked at me politely and respectfully: I might just as well have been speaking Greek.

ROBERT: Yeah, I know what you mean.

BRANDEN: What do you think that girl was feeling?

ROBERT: My folks did things like that. Still do. You feel so frustrated. You can't fight back; you don't have their weapons. How do you answer when they talk that way? What is there to answer, anyway? There's nothing to say. You just feel hurt, crushed, humiliated.

BRANDEN: And you feel utterly unreal to them. As though you don't really exist for them.

ROBERT: You can say that again. All you can do is make up your mind they're not going to get to you.

BRANDEN: What does that mean?

ROBERT: You make up your mind you won't care. You won't care about them. So whatever they say, it won't matter.

BRANDEN: How do you accomplish that?

ROBERT: You just tell yourself it's stupid to go on hoping that they'll understand you or treat you like you're a human being. It's too much to expect. As long as you're hoping for it, they have the power to disappoint you. To hurt you. So you stop hoping. Then you feel better.

BRANDEN: Do you?

ROBERT: I wonder why people act that way.

BRANDEN: They act that way because they're filled with hostility—a hostility they don't know how to handle or resolve. They feel hostile, because they feel frightened and helpless and out of control—and angry at the nameless people whom they blame for their condition. Incidentally, that's where their bad temper comes from, too. Perhaps—years earlier—they were hurt or frightened in their relationships with people, and they implicitly decided to repress it and not let themselves know what they felt, to drive their emotions underground, in order to permit themselves to believe that they were not suffering, that they were "in control," that they were on top of things. But the pain and the rage are still there. And they erupt at times. And if their children are in the way, that's tough for the children.

ROBERT: That's right. When my father throws a temper fit, you can see his weakness, you can see it's just weakness; he doesn't know what to do.

BRANDEN: That doesn't make it any more fun or any easier to bear when you're the target, does it?

ROBERT: You get used to it.

BRANDEN: No, you don't. You never get used to it. No one does. It's always a nightmare. It's always horrible. It's always wrong and cruel and unjust.

ROBERT: You're really making me feel lousy.

BRANDEN: Am I? Describe what you're feeling.

ROBERT: Everything is getting stirred up inside me. I feel weird.

BRANDEN: Perhaps you're feeling a bit anxious. That might be because thoughts and feelings you've repressed are struggling up to the surface of your mind.

ROBERT: What's the point of feeling these things? What's the use? What does it accomplish?

BRANDEN: That's one of the most harmful ideas people can entertain—"What's the point of feeling this emotion?" Emotions are value responses, automatic summations and reflections of your evaluations, of the meaning events have for you. When you try to turn off an emotion, to deny its reality, to block it out of your mind, what you're really doing, and what you're really trying to do, is to block out the *meaning* of the emotion, the value significance of the event to which the emotion is a response.

Those things happened in your life. They were important; they affected you. If you were badly hurt, it's desirable for you to know it; it's desirable for you to know how you evaluated the significance, and the implications for yourself, of your parents' manner of dealing with you. If you drew the conclusion that no one is to be trusted, you've got to identify that fact—so that you can rethink the matter on a conscious level. If you drew the conclusion that there must be something wrong with you to evoke such treatment, you've got to know that. Let's get it out into the open and ask ourselves whether that really is the right conclusion to draw.

But if you don't know what you felt, then you don't know what things meant to you, or mean to you now. You've denied yourself access to yourself. You've cut yourself off from the contents of your own mind.

ROBERT: I don't see what I gain by crying.

BRANDEN: You've been crying for eighteen years—without the relief of tears. The crying is there, inside you, and it's in your eyes. Every time I look at you, I can see the crying—even when you're laughing. So what are you talking about? It's already a fact. Who is being fooled? From whom are we keeping it a secret?

ROBERT: I hate weakness.

BRANDEN: Then stop being weak. Being afraid to face your own emotions—is that strength? Being afraid to acknowledge your own pain—is that heroic?

ROBERT: I don't want to fall to pieces.

BRANDEN: You won't fall to pieces. You'll sit here and you'll cry and you'll tell me what you feel and you'll suffer like hell and we'll talk about it, and eventually we'll get it all clear and you'll stop crying and you'll be free of all this—and you will have faced it like a man. Not like a boy who has to act tough to impress himself.

ROBERT: All right, all right, I'm crying. Satisfied?

BRANDEN: You're goddamn right I am.

Annihilation

Did your parents treat you with respect?

Were your thoughts, needs and feelings given consideration?

Was your dignity as a human being acknowledged?

When you expressed ideas or opinions, were they treated seriously?

Were your likes and dislikes treated seriously? (Not necessarily agreed with or acceded to, but nonetheless treated seriously?)

Were your desires treated thoughtfully and respectfully?

Client: Roger, twenty-two years old.

BRANDEN: Roger, the first of these questions is the basic one. The subsequent questions are merely offered as guides to illuminate what I'm after, and possibly to help stimulate your memory. You can respond to any of these questions you wish, or to all of them.

58

ROGER: Funny, when you first gave us the whole list of questions a few weeks ago, I really felt shook up. It felt like my emotions were running all over the place.

BRANDEN: And now?

ROGER: Now, I don't seem to feel anything.

BRANDEN: After the initial shock of the questions, you froze up. That often happens. At first the questions catch a person unprepared; they hit painful memories, and important thoughts and emotions begin to surface. Then the same repressive barrier that caused that material to get blocked in the first place starts swinging into action. The barrier drops again. And you're back in a deep freeze.

ROGER: My mind seems empty.

BRANDEN: We'll begin very factually. Don't expect to feel anything. Just tell me, yes or no, did your parents treat you with respect, in the sense I've indicated?

ROGER: Definitely not.

BRANDEN: How do you know?

ROGER: Huh?

BRANDEN: How do you know? If you know enough to say it with such certainty, you must remember something, some facts or events to support your statement. Begin there.

ROGER: As far as respect or dignity goes, there was very little shown me by my parents. I am one of six brothers and I was always treated as a "unit"— "one of the six boys." We were all treated that way. Never a response to me because I was me—anyway, none I can remember. I was always "one of the boys." A unit or a cipher, that's all.

Growing up was a constant process of struggling to be an adult or to reach maturity, so that I would be treated as a human being. Children were not human beings to my parents.

As far as my physical needs went, I was never so much as sent to bed without dinner as punishment. But if you mean psychological needs, my parents wouldn't have any knowledge of that. They wouldn't know what you're talking about.

BRANDEN: How would the lack of respect manifest itself?

ROGER: Talking about me as if I weren't in the room. Mother and Father discussing what they liked— or more often, didn't like—about me, as if I were not present. "Roger shouts too loud." "Roger might grow up with oversized ears." "Roger is more intelligent than Mark, but I don't think he's as smart as Jerry." "Roger is such a burden at times."

BRANDEN: What did that make you feel?

ROGER: That I had no importance.

BRANDEN: All right, go ahead.

ROGER: Never being spoken to with any sort of courtesy. My father would talk to a busboy in a restaurant with more politeness than he ever gave to me. Everything was an order. Never "please," never "thank you," or "if you don't mind," or anything like that. Just do this, do that, go here, go there, shut up, get out of the way, pick up this, carry that—orders, orders, orders. Just an object to be ordered around.

BRANDEN: You felt you didn't exist as a person.

ROGER: Just about.

BRANDEN: Most parents evidently don't realize that children are fully as deserving of courtesy and respect as adults. They're entitled to it and it's very important that they receive it—important to them psychologically. One of the ways a young child is taught to respect himself is through being treated with respect by others, through being treated as an entity worthy of respect. If he is treated as though he were an object undeserving of such consideration, the danger is that he may come to agree. And treat himself accordingly.

People often ask me what parents can do to encourage the development of healthy self-esteem in their children. Well, this is one major way.

ROGER: I have a horrible, empty feeling . . . the memory of having run to one or the other of my parents for attention when I was excited about something, and being sent away or even rebuffed. I wasn't sent away if I was hurt, but if I was happy, I generally was. Anyway, that's how I remember it.

Wait a minute, that's not quite right what I said about being hurt. It did apply, I think, when I was very young and if I fell and cut my knee or something. Then they'd pick me up, tend to my wounds. But if I were confused or if my pain were mental, they didn't know how to deal with it, or it wasn't real to them, or it had no importance—it didn't seem to have any importance. They would just tell me to be cheerful. "You'll have to learn to live with it," was one of Mom's favorite phrases. If I felt that she or Dad had mistreated me about something, or if I made any other kind of complaint, that would be her answer. It made me feel very hurt and frustrated, and very, very lonesome.

Many times I looked at Dad across the living room while he sat reading and I wanted to go sit on his lap. But I didn't go unless he asked me to and that was very seldom. The same thing with Mom; when she was washing dishes, I would sit in the kitchen and watch her and want very much to have her stop and hold me and talk to me. Just me—without the rest of my brothers—just me for a little while. I don't think it ever happened.

After a while, I repressed that desire—"You'll just have to learn to live with it."

Yes, and this: instructions from my folks not to show sadness and hurt feelings—which today I know means to repress them—made me think of those feelings as weak and, in some way, dirty, definitely undesirable. No one was to see me express them. My feelings had to be hidden. They would make me weak.

BRANDEN: What would happen when and if you expressed a desire—a desire to do something, or for some possession?

ROGER: Often, there was nothing, as if no one had spoken, as though nothing had been said. Or else my parents would simply answer, "We'll see," and I knew it had no importance for them whatsoever. They made all the decisions.

BRANDEN: So you had no sense of effectiveness in your relationship with them. You felt impotent.

ROGER: Oh, yes. Very helpless. Sometimes they would do things for me—buy me toys, or take me on an outing, or to a movie. But there was nothing personal about it, nothing for me, just specifically for me because *I* wanted it; but rather they did it because they must have realized that parents were supposed to do such things for their children. But they never did anything to imply that what I wanted was important, or that I was important. My feelings or desires couldn't have mattered less.

BRANDEN: It's very desirable today, for your own protection, that you realize how wrong they were, how unjust their manner of treating you, how disastrously they failed in their responsibilities as parents. The two most important things about us —about any of us—about human beings—are what we think and what we want. Our judgments and our values. A person's capacity to think and his capacity to desire are his two most valuable attributes.

ROGER: I feel as though I have no capacity to desire. I don't want anything, that's the problem. What for?

BRANDEN: The message was conveyed to you since the day you were born: your desires are insignificant, they don't count.

ROGER: And your thoughts are insignificant.

BRANDEN: Meaning: you're insignificant.

TED (another client): Then the child comes to agree and to begin having the same attitude toward his desires.

MARY (another client): And toward himself as a person.

ROGER: That's me.

BRANDEN: Very few people are able to retain into adulthood the ability to want anything passionately. Yet wanting things—and struggling to achieve them—is what life is all about.

ROGER: I was to be fed, clothed, sent to school, spanked, kissed goodnight and put to bed. What I thought or felt or wanted didn't make any difference. That was life at home. All of the kids got the same idea conveyed to them: the world is a place where what you want doesn't count. I concluded long ago that I shouldn't show feelings or initiate thoughts. They might be important to me, but they aren't to be expressed; they don't mean anything to anyone else and never can.

BRANDEN: Unfortunately, the truth is worse than that: your thoughts and feelings end up by not being important to you, either. And you gradually stop having them. And those you have, too often get repressed.

Your parents didn't treat you decently, granted. They didn't treat you with respect. They didn't take you seriously as a person. When they looked at you, they didn't see you. When you spoke, they didn't hear. But do you feel you have to go on treating yourself the same way? Do you feel you have no choice but to treat yourself without respect, and to treat your thoughts and feelings as unimportant?

ROGER: I'd like to break free of all that.

BRANDEN: Do you think you can?

ROGER: Well, I don't see any necessary reason why I should be screwed up forever over this.

BRANDEN: I don't either. But it's you who will have to do the changing. I'd like you to write a paper. We've just touched today on a small part of the childhood origins of your negative self-concept. I'd like to see how much farther you can carry it on your own. Study the whole list of questions, think about your childhood, think about your relationship with your parents, and see what you can come up with. See what you can identify about the factors that hurt you, that might have throttled your normal development. Here's something else to consider when you're working: don't think only about what they did to you, think about your own reactions; think about your own mental processes at the time. Consider the extent of your own possible complicity. Given your present passivity, it would be very easy for you to blame everything on your parents and thus to

perpetuate the delusion that you bear no responsibility for your own life or for the direction it
takes—or for the direction it is to take in the
future. Do you see what I mean?

ROGER: That would be like me, too. To feel that I was
just caught up in something I had no power over.
It lets me off the hook.

BRANDEN: Exactly. Remember: we're interested in the
way your parents treated you because we're interested in the conclusions you drew on the basis of
your experiences with your parents. It's what *you*
did that's really important. Never forget that. It's
not a matter of blame. But you don't serve your
own interests by seeing yourself as the passive
victim of fate.

ROGER: That's too easy.

BRANDEN: Much too easy. All right, think about it.
We'll move on to another question now.

The Dreamers

Did you feel that you were psychologically visible to your parents? Did you feel real to them?

Did your parents seem to make a genuine, thoughtful effort to understand you?

Did your parents seem authentically interested in you as a person?

Could you talk to your parents about issues of importance and receive interested, meaningful understanding from them?

Client: Laura, twenty-seven years old.

BRANDEN: This question may seem very similar to the one I asked about respect. But it's intended to focus on a somewhat different aspect of the parent-child relationship, although naturally there is some overlapping. Anyway, let's see what we get. Okay, Laura, let's work on this. What's your initial reaction?

LAURA: I think I'm a very lucky girl. Sitting here and listening to all these horrible stories, I feel, goodness me, I've been terribly fortunate. I don't have anything to blame my parents for.

BRANDEN: I'm not asking you to blame anyone. I merely want you to tell us what happened.

LAURA: You'll have to help me get started.

BRANDEN: You say you were lucky. Begin with that. Lucky in what way?

LAURA: Everyone in our house treated everyone else with respect. We were all trained to courtesy from the cradle. I never heard my mother or father raise their voice to anyone. I've never been so much as slapped; neither have my brothers or sisters. Heavens, it would have been inconceivable in our house.

We were all very well taken care of. All our needs were provided for. We were all dressed beautifully, and we were all taught excellent manners. My father always stood up when my mother came into the room. We were all taught to do that.

Mother was very cheerful; we would often hear her singing to herself.

From the time I was nine years old, I was permitted to attend adult parties, and I always had a new dress and Mother always took pains to see I looked pretty. Father took a great interest in my school work, as he did with the other children, and he would talk to our teachers personally and want to know everything that was going on in our lives. Everything was treated as important.

BRANDEN: What kind of parties?

LAURA: I beg your pardon?

BRANDEN: Tell me about the parties you attended.

LAURA: We have a large house and we did a lot of entertaining. I was the oldest of the children and Mother loved to show me off.

BRANDEN: How do you mean—show you off?

LAURA: You know, dress me up, fix my hair, and so forth.

BRANDEN: Was it enjoyable for you?

LAURA: Why, certainly.

BRANDEN: I wonder what a nine-year-old girl is doing, all dressed up, at a party for adults. I wonder how she feels.

LAURA: I was Mother's jewel, she said. What's the matter?

BRANDEN: I'm listening to you. I'm thinking.

LAURA: Well, you're making me uncomfortable.

BRANDEN: Tell me about your mother's singing.

LAURA: She would just go around the house humming to herself, humming all the time. Daddy would joke about it. The first thing he heard when he came home, he said, was Mama's humming.

BRANDEN: Do you know that you're not real right now, you're not real to yourself?

LAURA: I don't get what you're trying to say.

BRANDEN: Close your eyes, take a long, slow, deep breath, and relax. That's right, let all the tension go. Another deep breath. Fine. You're seven years old. Listen to your mother; she's moving through the house, humming. You're alone. What are you feeling?

LAURA: I—this is silly. . . . I'm afraid.

BRANDEN: Describe how it feels. Describe the fear.

LAURA: I don't know, it's. . . . I wish I could talk to Mother—I mean, sometime when I wanted to, and not just when she sat me down for a talk.

BRANDEN: Why can't you?

LAURA: Mama is busy. She has her own schedule. There's a time for everything, she always says.

BRANDEN: Keep your eyes closed. You're alone in the house with Mama. Go to her.

LAURA: She doesn't see me.

BRANDEN: Why not?

LAURA: She's sitting on the bed, going through some letters.

BRANDEN: Can't you talk to her?

LAURA: I don't know. I'm frightened. . . . Of course, I can talk to her. I can talk to her any time I want to. This is silly. I think I'm her favorite.

BRANDEN: She loves to show you off.

LAURA: What's wrong with that?

BRANDEN: Another deep breath. That's right. Tell me what you're feeling.

LAURA: I want to call out to her. I want Mama to hold me. I want her to hear me.

BRANDEN: Are you able to say why you're crying?

LAURA: Oh, this is silly. I feel so embarrassed, what's wrong with me? This is so silly.

BRANDEN: It's all right. Just hang on. Talk about what you feel.

LAURA: Well . . . well . . . I wish everything wasn't done by a schedule. I wish we could just be, you know, free. . . .

MARY (another client): I think—

BRANDEN: Not now, Mary.

LAURA: I wish I knew why I felt so strange.

BRANDEN: It's like being behind a glass wall, isn't it? You want to reach out, but you can't. No one can see you. No one can hear you. Is that what you feel?

MARY: That's just what I wanted to say. I know that feeling.

BRANDEN: Sorry. You're doing fine, Laura.

LAURA: I guess . . . everything was . . . was an idea inside Mama and Papa's mind. . . . What does that mean? What does it mean, what I just said?

BRANDEN: Can anyone help Laura?

MARY: Her parents weren't real. That's what it sounds like. They weren't real to themselves: they were disconnected. Their bodies were in this world and their heads were in a dream world, and their bodies were being pulled by strings from that other world.

LAURA: I was Mama's "jewel." Dick was Papa's "big boy." Jenny was "little flower." Edgar was . . . oh, something else, I can't remember.

BRANDEN: It would be very terrible to be only an idea, only a dream, inside your parents' private dream-world.

TED: Christ, we're all that.

LAURA: It's frightening. How can you talk about it? What is it? You can't get hold of it. It's a feeling.

TED: It's a nightmare.

BRANDEN: It sure as hell is a nightmare.

LAURA: I feel like I want to scream. I always wanted to scream.

BRANDEN: I think we can see why.

LAURA: I don't understand how you understand any of this. It's all so ... unclear. I'm just rambling.

BRANDEN: Everyone in this room understands it. It's not that difficult. Most important of all, you understand it, or you're beginning to.

LAURA: Could we—could I—would it be all right if we had a private appointment this week? I couldn't stand waiting till next Wednesday.

BRANDEN: We'll talk about it after group today. I probably should push you further, but, all right, I'll let you rest now.

Zero

Did you feel loved and valued by your parents, in the sense that you experienced yourself as a source of pleasure to them? Or did you feel unwanted, perhaps a burden? Or did you feel hated? Or did you feel you were simply an object of indifference?

Client: Alan, twenty-five years old.

BRANDEN: Alan, before we get into your answer to this question, let's pause a moment and consider what's involved.

We hear so much about the importance of parents loving their children—as though, if parents only love their children, everything else will take care of itself. I think we've already seen that it won't. There's much more than love to successful child-raising. Such as all the things contained and implied in this list of questions we're working on. However, love is important, so let's talk about that. I want you to notice that I added a phrase, when I gave you the question a minute ago, that was not contained in my original formulation several weeks ago. The phrase I added was: "in the sense that you experienced yourself as a source of pleasure to them." I added this in order to make clear what I mean by being loved and valued.

ALAN: That was very helpful for me.

BRANDEN: Many clients don't have a clear concept of exactly what it would mean to be loved and valued. To love a person is to see in him the embodiment of one's own important, deeply held values, and also—I want to stress this—to perceive him as a source of pleasure. This applies to any kind of love, not only the love of a parent for a child. Its application is obvious in romantic love. But even if we talk about loving a new car or a piece of music, contained in what we mean is that the object of our love is a source of pleasure to us. This is essential to the meaning of love.

ALAN: But I'd like to know—why is it so important whether or not your parents love you?

BRANDEN: We'll let that emerge from our discussion. I have a feeling you're trying to stall.

ALAN: I have a feeling that I am, too.

BRANDEN: Okay. It means this question is going to get us somewhere.

ALAN: I would say that my parents loved me, except that they never took pleasure in anything, including me.

BRANDEN: How do you know they loved you?

ALAN: They were always concerned about my health. They would be worried if I came home late.

BRANDEN: You want to put me to work today, eh? Why are you giving me this nonsense? You know that what you're saying has nothing necessarily to do with love.

ALAN: I just feel so tired.

BRANDEN: And you know what that means, so let's go.

ALAN: I wanted my father to accept my interests, to care about what I was doing, not always to treat me as an alien—but he never did. I wasn't his kind of person. I would have to say that he considered me a burden. Sometimes he looked at me as if he hated me, but not often. Mother always tried to bring us together. She would overpraise me, especially when he was around.

BRANDEN: Did you feel that she loved you?

ALAN: She was always so worn out, so drained—who knew what she loved?

BRANDEN: Do you remember her ever picking you up, hugging you, saying you're her wonderful boy— you know, that kind of thing. Expressing pleasure at the sight of you?

ALAN: If she ever did, I can't remember it. Everything was just sort of . . . empty. I mean, in the house.

I mean, in the home atmosphere. There was no life.

BRANDEN: You must have felt very lonely.

ALAN: I feel dizzy and shaky right now.

BRANDEN: Don't be afraid of it. It's a signal we can use. It means we're on to something. What thoughts occur to you?

ALAN: Thoughts about my father. . . . What would he do if he knew I were discussing him in group? I've built up a fear of talking about it. . . . So much of what I did was to appease my father and to gain his approval. I'm afraid if I dig too deeply into this issue I'll probably come to the realization that for myself I haven't ever really wanted anything.

A couple of years ago, after I dropped one interest, I couldn't pick up anything else. I just couldn't do it. Maybe I was being honest then. I don't pursue things for myself. And whenever I'm just about to succeed, I stop. Everything suddenly comes to a halt, and it all feels useless and beside the point. Whether it's the pursuit of a job or a girl or anything. Maybe the honest thing is to admit it and not to pretend, not to go after anything.

BRANDEN: How does it feel, when you're at the point of stopping—of giving up, of abandoning your goal?

ALAN: Like it's meaningless. Success would be a farce or a fake.

BRANDEN: A fake because you know you're worthless?

ALAN: Yes:

BRANDEN: Were you born feeling worthless?

ALAN: No.

BRANDEN: Were you worthless by the time you were five years old?

ALAN: Yes.

BRANDEN: All right, then, we know where to look. You became worthless, in your own eyes, somewhere between the age of one minute and five years.

ALAN: The word that comes into my mind is "protection."

BRANDEN: Go ahead.

ALAN: My father would laugh at me. He wouldn't consider me a real boy. He wouldn't have seen me as being like him. And whenever I'm about to succeed, I can see him laughing at me, saying that I'll never make it, not really—the success won't be real, it won't last, it can't be happening to me.

BRANDEN: So giving up is protecting yourself against the pain of his laughter, since you're going to be defeated anyway?

ALAN: I'm not sure, but that feels right. Yes, I think that's right.

BRANDEN: It's on the right track, but it doesn't go deep enough.

ALAN: I wasn't born feeling worthless; I suppose I was born feeling I was good.

BRANDEN: You weren't born having any opinion of yourself. That comes later. But I think the natural state of a human organism is a primitive feeling of self-affirmation. At least, at the beginning. The natural state of a conscious, living organism is to value itself. I'm thinking of a young puppy or a kitten. Doesn't it take its value for granted? Isn't that part of the charm and attractiveness of a young animal? Or of a baby. A baby that hasn't yet been given the sense of having been born into a nightmare.

ALAN: Why can't that feeling last, in human beings?

BRANDEN: Nature may give human beings a start in the right direction—by that primitive sense of self-value we're talking about—but to be kept and developed, self-value has to be earned; it has to be achieved through the individual's own volitional efforts, through becoming a rational, self-responsible being. And here's where parents can help: by treating the child as a value, by confirming the child's best sense of himself and encouraging him to build on it, to acquire a mature self-esteem.

ALAN: But if the parents don't——

BRANDEN: It can be very bewildering to a young child. The world doesn't make sense. He feels proud of his growing control over his body, of his

growing skills, but his parents don't respond;
they're indifferent or unconcerned or even impatient or hostile, and this runs against the child's
own sense of things—of the way things should
be—and is, in effect, disorienting to the child,
and perhaps the child begins to put his own
understanding in question.

ALAN: How would a two-year-old child possibly be
able to cope with the feeling that he's an object
of hatred?

BRANDEN: It would be pretty difficult, wouldn't it?

ALAN: The child couldn't possibly survive it.

BRANDEN: Some children do. Their will to understand,
their will to efficacy—which I discussed in *The
Psychology of Self-Esteem*—carries them through.
But for some children, it's just too much to
handle.
It's beside the point, right now, to worry about
whether or not your responses to your parents'
manner of dealing with you were avoidable. The
fact is, those were your responses. Let's try to
understand them.

ALAN: I hero-worshipped my father. He was very
strong; he had a deep voice. He always seemed
sure of himself.

BRANDEN: What did it mean, that he didn't love you?
Or that he didn't seem to love you?

ALAN: That I wasn't a man.

BRANDEN: You respected your father. Therefore, you respected his judgment. If you hadn't seen values in him, values you admired, he probably wouldn't have had the same power to hurt you.

ALAN: That's right, that's definitely right. . . . When I was seven or eight, I was walking and holding hands with some boy, and my father looked at me strangely and said something that I understood as meaning that I was doing something wrong or strange. Also, he seemed disappointed that I didn't get into more fights, and when I got into them and didn't win, it made him furious. I was no son of his.

BRANDEN: Let's go back to your mother.

ALAN: I just felt I didn't matter. She'd feed and clothe and take care of me, but like a machine. She was a machine and I was a machine.

BRANDEN: You felt very hopeless about it all. You still do.

ALAN: I feel that I'm . . . nothing. Everything is a fake. Everything that isn't nothing about me is a pretense. I'm acting all the time.

BRANDEN: Including right now.

ALAN: How do you mean?

BRANDEN: I wish I had a recording of this. I'd like you to hear your tone of voice.

HELEN (another client): It's all a cry for sympathy. We're supposed to feel sorry for you.

ERNEST (another client): You're still five years old.

ALAN: Why is everyone picking on me?

BRANDEN: Is that how you perceive it?

ALAN: No, I don't stand by that.

BRANDEN: There might be two reasons for their attitude. One is the suspicion that you're playing for pity. The other is that the things you're talking about are triggering off pain in them, and they don't like it.

ALAN: Anyway, my parents treated me like nothing, and as you say, I agreed with them.

BRANDEN: However parents choose to deal with a child, they are implicitly conveying a message of how they estimate him. If they're indifferent, they're communicating the message that he is negligible, unimportant, without value. If they project hatred, they communicate the message that he is a disvalue, that he is bad, undesirable, evil.

ALAN: I got it all, and accepted it all.

BRANDEN: And internalized it all. Made it a part of yourself. Assimilated it into your self-concept. Worse than that, built your self-concept out of it.

NANCY (another client): Why is he always trying to gain everyone's sympathy?

ALAN: Because I don't feel I have anything to offer. No positive values.

BRANDEN: How are you feeling?

ALAN: This is funny. I feel much better.

BRANDEN: Good, but it won't last.

ALAN: Why not?

BRANDEN: You feel better—in part—because of the attention that's being paid to you.

ALAN: That's true.

BRANDEN: But you're not really thinking about what we're discussing. You're very passive and listless. Your brain is inactive. I can see it on your face. So when you leave here, or within an hour or two, or a day or two, the depression will come back. Because you're not doing anything to fight it. You're not thinking.

ALAN: But, you know, I feel something is changing. Something inside me. I'm not trying to make excuses, because everything you're saying is true, but I do feel this is doing me good. It's hard to describe, but I feel that some change in perspective is taking place inside me, a little bit at a time, like reality is getting to me, in spite of——

BRANDEN: In spite of your inertia?

ALAN: I guess so.

BRANDEN: That's good, but it's not good enough. We have to push harder. You have to push harder.

ALAN: I've given up any hope of achieving self-esteem, haven't I? I mean, a long time ago. That's the negative self-concept: that I'm a failure, that I always was a failure and always will be. I can't succeed; that wouldn't be me. It wouldn't be in character. That's what's holding me down, that view of myself.

BRANDEN: And your father's laughter is just the externalized symbol of that.

ALAN: Hey—now I *really* feel better. No fooling.

BRANDEN: Is this real?

ALAN: As far as I can tell, it is—at least, right now.

BRANDEN: Okay, it's a beginning. Unfortunately, we've run out of time. To be continued.

The Sinner

Did your parents deal with you fairly and justly?

Did your parents resort to threats in order to control your behavior—either threats of immediate punitive action on their part, or threats in terms of long-range consequences for your life, or threats of supernatural punishments, such as going to hell?

Were you praised when you performed well? Or merely criticized when you performed badly?

Were your parents willing to admit it when they were wrong? Or was it against their policy to concede that they were wrong?

Client: Jane, thirty-four years old.

BRANDEN: Perhaps I should remind everyone once again that although I speak of "your parents," the answer to these questions will not necessarily be identical for both parents and that you may want to respond differently for each parent.

JANE: I understand.

BRANDEN: Let me take a minute longer to review our
purpose here. When I first gave these questions
to this group and to my other groups, a number
of participants said that they had considerable
difficulty in working on the questions at home—
difficulty in knowing how to answer the questions. Some people felt that the questions had no
real bearing on their problems and would not be
useful. So, to demonstrate the value of the questions, to show you the kind of information they
can elicit, and to provide more detailed direction
on how to work with them, I proposed that I
would work on at least one question with each
member of each group.

Let me stress again, because this cannot be
overemphasized, that you are not your parents'
psychological creation; to a major extent, you are
your own psychological creation. The purpose of
this inquiry is not to give you the opportunity to
blame everything that is wrong with you on your
parents. That in most cases your parents failed
miserably in their responsibilities toward you is
undeniably true. But what we are concerned
with here are the emotions you experienced in
response to their behavior and the conclusions
you drew which may still be affecting you.

What I especially want you to pay attention to as
we proceed is the relevance of your parents'
manner of dealing with you to the formation of
your negative self-concept—to the extent that
your self-concept *is* negative.

A negative self-concept consists of the view or
attitude or feeling that one is essentially immoral
or sinful or depraved or inadequate or stupid or
ineffectual or inferior or mediocre or worthless.

Many factors went into the formation of your
negative self-concept, of which parental treat-

ment was only one. But that is the aspect we are choosing to explore right now.

KEITH (another client): Even though you haven't worked on a question with me yet, I feel I've benefited a great deal just from sitting here and watching and listening. I've made a lot of notes; in fact, I'm writing a long paper on the things I've learned that are applicable to me.

BRANDEN: Good. What has the net effect been on you so far?

KEITH: The sense of becoming more intelligible to myself. The knowledge that there are reasons why I developed as I did.

JANE: I'd like to begin by responding to the last part of the question. My mother and father were never wrong. There was no such thing as them being wrong. There was God in heaven and here on earth there was my mother and father. I suppose God doesn't admit His mistakes, either.

BRANDEN: Did you ever confront either of your parents with the belief that they made a mistake about something, judged the situation incorrectly or treated you unfairly or whatever?

JANE: Not that I can remember. It would have been a suicide mission, anyway. I grew up on a farm in Minnesota. My only relief was to run away into the woods for a little while, just to be by myself.

BRANDEN: Relief from what?

JANE: From being yelled at or hit or told I was no
     good. My father would ask me to do something
     and I would do it, and then he would say he had
     asked me to do something else and get angry at
     me. If I would try to argue, Mother would snap
     at me not to talk back to Father. If I tried to
     argue with Mother, Father would tell me I had
     to learn respect for my elders. There was no
     justice, no fairness, no reasoning with them, no
     way to be heard. I tried to keep out of their way.

BRANDEN: Did either of your parents ever praise you
     for anything you did? Did they ever compliment
     you?

JANE: Never. The only time I existed was when I did
     did something wrong.

BRANDEN: Then they would pay attention to you.

JANE: Yes.

BRANDEN: What kind of thing did you do wrong?

JANE: Forgetting to feed the animals. Spilling some-
     thing. Not doing well in some subject at school.

BRANDEN: Then what happened?

JANE: I think Father hated me. I think he really hated
     me. When he looked at me and he was angry, his
     eyes would blaze—as if it took all his control not
     to kill me.

BRANDEN: Did he have a temper?

JANE: A terrible temper. And you never knew what would cause him to flare up. His word was law: he was judge, jury and executioner. The farm was his kingdom and he was the absolute ruler. I really wanted him to love me. Maybe I'm being unfair. Maybe there's another side to him I don't know about.

BRANDEN: You're feeling sorry for him?

JANE: Yes ... I think I am.

BRANDEN: I don't think so, I think you're using that as a cover-up—to keep from getting angry.

JANE: If one of us did something wrong, he'd often punish all of the children. He'd justify it by saying, "If you haven't done anything wrong yet, you will later. This is a sample of what you can expect." He was an ignorant man, with very little education—and afraid of people who were educated, I remember that.

BRANDEN: Is he dead?

JANE: No—he's still on the farm. Yelling at somebody, I'm sure.

BRANDEN: You spoke of him in the past tense.

JANE: Does that mean I wish he were dead?

BRANDEN: Maybe, but I took it somewhat differently. I felt it was a way of keeping him distant from you—disassociated from your present context.

JANE: It was really painful, growing up that way.

BRANDEN: Go on.

JANE: He was terribly autocratic.

BRANDEN: What are you trying to avoid saying?

JANE: Nothing. I . . . Mother was a terror, too. She hardly ever spoke to me except to tell me I was wrong or had done something wrong or was a bad girl or God would punish me.

BRANDEN: What did that make you feel?

JANE: Helpless and hopeless. There was no way to win their approval. Nothing I could do would make any difference. If I acted properly, it wouldn't be noticed. I wouldn't hear anything from them—until I did something wrong.

BRANDEN: Tell me how your mother would criticize you.

JANE: If I wanted to play in the orchard when she needed me for something, she'd call me a sinner. No kidding. A sinner. I didn't have to do anything really wrong, it could be just about anything at all, anything that displeased her. Her eyes were so bitter. She told me I was God's curse on her. I suspect I was an accident. I can never remember a time when I didn't feel guilty. I think I was born feeling guilty.

BRANDEN: Were you often physically punished?

JANE: Yes.

BRANDEN: Were you told, in effect, that you'd come to a bad end? That a terrible fate was in store for you?

JANE: Yes.

BRANDEN: What about supernatural punishment?

JANE: Can you imagine telling a five-year-old girl that the flames of hell will eat her flesh through all eternity? Because she took a piece of cake she wasn't supposed to have?

BRANDEN: What does the little girl feel?

JANE: Terror.

BRANDEN: What else?

JANE: Bewilderment.

BRANDEN: What else?

JANE: Rage?

BRANDEN: Are you asking me or telling me?

JANE: I'm telling you, I guess.

BRANDEN: What else?

JANE: I'm not important to anyone. I have no value.

BRANDEN: What else?

JANE: Isn't that enough?

BRANDEN: What else?

JANE: You're making me cry.

BRANDEN: What else?

JANE: Of course, speaking as an adult, I really think I am a bad person.

BRANDEN: Tell me about it. Bad in what way?

JANE: Well, I tried to kill my father when I was thirteen.

BRANDEN: That's what you didn't want to tell me before, isn't it?

JANE: Yes.

BRANDEN: What did you actually do?

JANE: I came into his bedroom with a pitchfork when he was sleeping.

BRANDEN: And then?

JANE: I couldn't stab him. I got out before he woke up.

BRANDEN: Is that all?

JANE: I was very promiscuous sexually for some years.

BRANDEN: What do you mean by "promiscuous"?

JANE: I went with a lot of men. Some of them were awful—I didn't care. It made me feel dirty. I still feel that way.

BRANDEN: How many is "a lot"?

JANE: Over twenty.

BRANDEN: You started feeling dirty long before you knew what sex was.

JANE: True. Still, that made me feel pretty bad.

BRANDEN: Did it? Why?

JANE: Don't you condemn sexual promiscuity?

BRANDEN: We're not discussing me, we're discussing you. Explain why it's wrong.

JANE: I don't understand you.

BRANDEN: Look, I won't argue about the undesirability of sexual promiscuity. Of course it's wrong. It's degrading psychologically. It means acting blindly, out of fear, without reason or judgment or standards. It is not, however, a capital crime. There are a few worse things in this world.

JANE: Such as what?

BRANDEN: Such as threatening five-year-old girls with hell.

JANE: I did other bad things.

BRANDEN: For instance?

JANE: In my adolescence, sometimes I was mean. I
    could be very unpleasant—you know, sarcastic. I
    became rebellious, and I would deliberately do
    things I knew would infuriate my parents. I
    didn't care.

BRANDEN: I suspect that you cared very much. You
    wanted to infuriate them. That's why you did it.
    So they would pay attention to you.

JANE: That's true.

BRANDEN: If parents ignore children when they per-
    form well, but criticize them when they act badly,
    do you know what message they're conveying?
    That the way to get attention is to act badly. It's
    the only thing that will work. Acting well brings
    one nothing, so far as other people are concerned.
    I worked with a client who took drugs and con-
    trived to be caught by the police so that he would
    at least win his parents' attention.

JANE: I can understand that.

BRANDEN: I know you can.

JANE: I did a great many wrong things, just to get a
    reaction, just to feel that I existed. If people
    scream at you, they know you're there.

BRANDEN: I wonder how satisfying that is.

JANE: Not very.

BRANDEN: If you praise a child's behavior when it's
    good, and condemn his behavior when it's bad—I
    mean, praise and condemn in rational terms,

without phony enthusiasm and without overse-
verity—you give the child the priceless sense of
living in a just universe. The responses he re-
ceives are understandable to him. There is a
logical, cause-and-effect relationship between his
actions and the responses he elicits. And further,
by dealing with him that way, treating him fairly
and justly, you're teaching him how he should
deal with other people.

JANE: I can't even imagine what that would be like.

BRANDEN: If all you ever hear from your parents is
that you're bad, then that's their contribution to
your self-concept, to the extent that they have an
effect on you.

JANE: They had an effect.

BRANDEN: I know. The tragedy is that you begin by
accepting an unearned guilt—and then you proceed to earn it.

JANE: How do you mean?

BRANDEN: Don't you see? You were pounded with the
message that you were worthless. You accepted
and absorbed it. But then, why aspire to be
virtuous? Why preserve moral standards? It's
useless, you're no good anyway. So when you're
tempted to do things you know are not right,
why resist? What's the point? What are you holding out for? There is nothing to preserve. That
very feeling of being bad, of being wrong as a
person, of being evil, will tend to generate irrational desires—because one will not feel fit for or
worthy of the good. Then, when you experience

the desires, you tell yourself, "You see, my parents were right, I am evil." And then you proceed to act on those desires and again you tell yourself, "You see, they *really* were right, I *really* am evil." You keep reinforcing their message—and you keep reinforcing your own negative self-concept.

JANE: The fact remains, I am bad.

BRANDEN: Because of the promiscuity? Do you think that makes you evil? I don't. It was stupid of you; it was irrational, it was weak, it was self-destructive. But if you're going to call that evil, what moral designation will you reserve for a mass murderer?

JANE: I don't know. . . .

BRANDEN: Your guilt—if you're eager to feel guilty about something—is that you've spent so much of your life not thinking—not attempting to judge your parents or evaluate their behavior, not attempting to achieve a rational life for yourself. You surrendered to unthinking fear and guilt as a child, and you've been riding your emotions blindly ever since.

As to the promiscuity—you were a frightened, lonely girl who has felt rejected all her life. And so you wanted some experience of human closeness—of warmth, of relating to someone—and you wanted to feel that you were important to someone, that you had value for someone, that someone cared about you. So you chose sex as your means of obtaining that experience. Was it a good idea? Of course not. Did it work? Of course not. Was it moral? No—because you had to turn off your mind in order to do it. But do you really think you deserve to be condemned to hell for it? For the promiscuity? Don't be absurd. You need to be told to stop treating yourself so shabbily— to have more respect for your own life, and to start functioning as a thinking being.

JANE: But when you hate yourself, you can really act like a bitch.

BRANDEN: Are you trying to convince me that you're too rotten to change? That can be a great escape, you know. Of course you've acted like a bitch. And so long as you continue to see yourself as a bitch, you'll go on acting like one.

JANE: That's so true.

BRANDEN: The first step of achieving moral stature is to commit oneself to one's own moral potential.

JANE: You'll have to convince me.

BRANDEN: Of what?

JANE: Of my moral potential.

BRANDEN: Okay, we'll fight about it.

JANE: I don't know whether I feel better or worse. I'm beginning to get a glimmer of what happened. It's slowly becoming real to me.

BRANDEN: Good.

JANE: Wouldn't it be funny if I weren't evil?

BRANDEN: It would be very funny.

Parental Love and Other Tragedies

Was it your parents' practice to punish you or discipline you by striking or beating you?

Client: Roy, twenty-eight years old.

BRANDEN: What's your story, Roy?

ROY: I wouldn't say I was struck a great deal, except maybe in the first few years. By adolescence, I was no longer being hit.

BRANDEN: Who did the hitting?

ROY: My father; never my mother.

BRANDEN: Tell us about it.

ROY: My father had a certain theory of punishment. It wasn't just a question of hitting me or one of the other kids; it was the way it was done. Suppose I was at the supper table and was making too much noise—maybe I'd been told to be quiet one or two times before. My father would wait until my head was turned away from him, so that I couldn't see what he was doing, then he would reach out and wallop me and yell at me to stop it—the blow and the shout coming in the same instant.

BRANDEN: What was the idea behind that?

ROY: My father felt—and he explained this in so many words years later—that if the punishment were combined with an element of surprise, of shock, the impact would be greater. In other words, it would be more terrifying. He was right, too; it was more terrifying, and I seldom disobeyed him more than twice on the same issue.

BRANDEN: You were frightened of him.

ROY: All the time. I think he wanted me to be. That was part of his notion of discipline. He would tell me: "You'll spend most of your life having to take orders, so you might as well start learning now."

BRANDEN: So your education in "taking orders" began shortly after birth.

ROY: As far back as I can remember.

BRANDEN: What do you think was the effect of this treatment on you?

ROY: I don't know, that's hard to say. It subdued me. It made me feel I wanted to hide.

BRANDEN: Hide from whom?

ROY: From everyone.

BRANDEN: There was a spread effect. Everyone became potentially frightening to you.

ROY: Yes.

BRANDEN: Are you still hiding?

ROY: I guess so.

BRANDEN: You're very mild-mannered and emotionally flat during this conversation. Are you hiding right now?

ROY: Yes, in a way. There's always the fear that I'll say something that won't be approved of and then . . . I don't know what.

BRANDEN: I want you to imagine that there's a two-month-old puppy right here, sitting on the floor. Right now, it's full of life and energy, and it's absolutely fearless—the way a living entity should be. Now let's imagine that we proceed to treat it the way your father treated you. We'll start scaring the hell out of it. We'll look for occasions to shock it, to hit it really hard, to hurt it and startle it in as many ways as we can, always catching it unprepared, so that it never knows when the blow and the shout are coming. It hears "No!" and "Bad!" constantly. Keep at it that way. Now it's several months later—

ROY: Oh, stop it! . . .

BRANDEN: What's the matter?

ROY: This is too upsetting. It's awful.

BRANDEN: Sure it's awful. That's the point. It's monstrous. It's cruel, what we're doing to the dog, isn't it? It's barbaric.

ROY: Yes.

BRANDEN: If it's done to a child?

ROY: It's wrong.

BRANDEN: Is that the strongest word you can use?

ROY: It's very wrong.

BRANDEN: Then how should we appraise an adult human being who treats a child that way?

ROY: He's a rotten person.

BRANDEN: Yes, he is. He's cruel. Whether he knows it or not, he's behaving like a cruel bastard. Isn't that true?

ROY: Yes.

BRANDEN: Is it real to you?

ROY: I think so.

BRANDEN: All right now, let's consider the state of that dog after six months of such treatment.

ROY: It would be huddled under the couch, afraid to come out, afraid to make a move, afraid of everything.

BRANDEN: Like you.

ROY: Like me.

BRANDEN: Two weeks ago, I was in San Francisco on business, and I met a former client of mine. I told him about the book I was writing on this list of questions and on the way we used these questions in therapy, and I mentioned that I hadn't yet found the right title for the book. He proposed a beauty. I'm not going to use it, but do you want to know what it is? *Parental Love and Other Tragedies.*

ROY: That's perfect.

BRANDEN: There are many parents who doubtless "love" their children—whatever the hell that word means to them—who have no better notion of how to educate their children than by subjecting them to physical violence. It's such a confession of intellectual bankruptcy and incompetence.

ROY: What does it prove?

BRANDEN: Exactly. All it proves is that the parents are bigger and stronger, which the child knows anyway.

ROY: It might make the child want to grow up in a hurry so that he can be big and strong and use physical violence against others in order to impose his wishes.

BRANDEN: Right. And there's an interesting point here. If people are appalled by the resurgence of violence which is occurring all over the world, if people wish to encourage the policy that differences should be settled peacefully, by reason rather than by force, isn't the raising of children the place to begin?

ROY: I took violence for granted.

BRANDEN: Too many people take violence for granted. They regard it as the normal.

ROY: There were a lot of other things, besides hitting me, that my father did.

BRANDEN: I would think so. The behavior you've been describing doesn't take place out of context and in isolation. It's part of a pattern; it's part of his total way of dealing with people.

ROY: Most of the time, when he wasn't hitting me or yelling at me, he was closed, remote, inaccessible.

BRANDEN: Which communicated what message to you?

ROY: I'm not important, I'm not worth bothering with.

BRANDEN: Do you think that was a reasonable conclusion for you to accept?

ROY: Today? No.

BRANDEN: You're generally very silent in group. It's difficult to get you to talk.

ROY: I always feel: suppose I say something stupid and wrong.

BUSINESS REPLY CARD

FIRST CLASS PERMIT NO. 4596   BEVERLY HILLS, CA.

POSTAGE WILL BE PAID BY ADDRESSEE

THE BIOCENTRIC INSTITUTE
P.O. BOX 4009
BEVERLY HILLS, CA. 90213

You are cordially invited...

... to join Nathaniel Branden at his Self-Esteem Intensive Workshops- (SELF-ESTEEM AND THE ART OF BEING, SELF-ESTEEM AND ROMANTIC RELATIONSHIPS and SELF-ESTEEM AND TRANSFORMATION) offered in major cities throughout the United States.

For free information about Dr. Branden's Intensives, return this postage-paid card.

Name _____

Address _____

City _____ State _____ Zip _____

BRANDEN: Do you think you could make an effort to live dangerously—to speak out more, even if it frightens you for a while?

ROY: I could try.

BRANDEN: You'll like yourself more if you do. It's very humiliating to keep surrendering to fear, isn't it?

ROY: Terribly.

BRANDEN: That's how you keep making the problem worse.

ROY: I know.

BRANDEN: Make an effort and let's see what happens. We'll want to explore this further—working out a strategy to help you start acting against your fears. We're not going to solve this problem simply by gaining insight into its roots. It has to be solved, in the last analysis, by action—by changing your behavior *now*. That will help generate a positive feedback to your self-concept, countering the negative feedback and reinforcement generated by your past surrenders to fear. Do you understand?

ROY: Sure. *Parental Love and Other Tragedies.* Great.

The Gambler

Did your parents project that they believed in your basic goodness? Or did they project that they saw you as bad or worthless or evil?

Client: Tony, thirty-one years old.

BRANDEN: What's your answer, Tony?

TONY: They made me feel bad, both of them. I could never do anything right. Many times Ma locked me in a closet for doing something wrong, and left me there for hours. I was frightened that she'd forget about me being there. It was dark and I just sat on the floor and waited and cried an awful lot, but no one ever came.

BRANDEN: Go on.

TONY: I got beat quite a bit by my father. My mother, sometimes. What was crazy was that at a certain point I would almost like it—you know, masochistic feelings; also, I began having sadistic fantasies. ... I liked both. ...

BRANDEN: You must have felt important to them when they were hitting you.

TONY: That's it, that's about the only time I did.

BRANDEN: So being hit was a form of having your existence and importance acknowledged. If you couldn't make an impression with your goodness, you could at least make an impression with your badness.

TONY: That was easy enough. As I say, I never could do anything right. I would work very hard washing my father's car—I swear it would be spotless—but then he would come out and find the one thing wrong, maybe a smudge of dirt under a fender. He wouldn't comment on the rest, on how good it looked, only on the one place where he found some dirt. Whatever I tried to do, it was always like that. It got so I'd wait, feeling quite a bit of fear, for him to find the one thing wrong on some job I had done. He would always find it.

BRANDEN: What did that make you feel?

TONY: That I was bad, that it would always be that way, that there was something wrong with me.

BRANDEN: I wonder why you experienced it as a moral reflection on yourself, rather than simply as a reflection on your competence.

TONY: Because of their attitude. They seemed to see it as a defect of my character, so I did too. I was always in trouble at school. I was a real trouble-maker. Always getting bawled out by the teachers or the principal. I was a wise guy.

BRANDEN: Do you think you did that to draw attention to yourself?

TONY: Probably. It was the only way I could get it.
I still get those negative messages from my parents whenever I see them. Nothing has changed.

BRANDEN: You felt everyone saw you as bad, and you acted out that role.

TONY: Yes.

BRANDEN: When did you begin stealing?

TONY: You mean, the small change from my father ...?

BRANDEN: No. Real stealing.

TONY: In my adolescence. In high school.

BRANDEN: And gambling?

TONY: Since I was a little kid.

BRANDEN: Did you ever think about why you did it?

TONY: No, it just felt natural.

BRANDEN: You know what I think? I think very early in life you concluded that you would never be able to obtain the things you wanted by honest effort. You were a loser.

TONY: I sure felt that.

BRANDEN: Also, you were bad. Not like other people. Not part of the human race, not capable of achieving your goals by the same process of work that enables other people to achieve theirs.

TONY: That's right.

BRANDEN: So you felt that if you were to get anything you wanted, it would have to be by stealing or by luck.

TONY: Hey, that's fantastic. It sounds right. I think that's right. I don't hardly steal anymore, except maybe postage stamps from the place where I work—little things like that, nothing big. Gambling is the thing now, and I've lost thousands of dollars.

BRANDEN: Most gamblers lose, as you know. Almost all of them. In the long run. But in your case—and this is very common—you want to lose, you don't want to win. You probably do things to make yourself lose.

TONY: How in hell did you know that?

BRANDEN: When you're winning you do something really stupid, don't you? Something you know better than to do. Some impulsive act that runs counter to everything you know about gambling strategy.

TONY: Always, goddamnit. Even for gambling, there are certain rules, percentages to follow and so forth. When the chips start piling up, I start forgetting everything I know and acting really crazy. I hate myself afterward and I feel fear in advance, because I know it's going to happen and I can't seem to control it. It drives me wild. Why do I do that?

BRANDEN: You're acting in accordance with your negative self-concept. Your deepest premise is that you're a loser, that you'll always be defeated. Gambling is a metaphysical drama. At least, that's what it seems to be for most gamblers. How will fate treat me? Is fate on my side or against me? Since you believe you're doomed to defeat, the anxiety starts building as soon as you start winning—because you feel it can't last, it's against your nature, you're not one of life's winners, you're one of life's losers. The anxiety goes on building and becomes intolerable, and so to put an end to it you precipitate your own defeat. Losing is more tolerable than the anxious anticipation of losing. It's waiting for the axe to fall that's unbearable. So you pull the string to let the axe fall yourself.

TONY: Do you think I'm trying to punish myself?

BRANDEN: That's the standard explanation one often hears. How does it strike you?

TONY: It doesn't do anything to me in particular. Just something I've heard.

BRANDEN: It's not impossible that that factor could be involved, but I don't see any necessity to introduce such an hypothesis. One can explain what you do without it.

TONY: What you're saying strikes me better. All I can say is, it feels true, there's a sense of recognition of what you're saying.

BRANDEN: You do experience that anxiety when you're winning?

TONY: Definitely.

BRANDEN: And it's relieved as soon as you lose?

TONY: Yes.

BRANDEN: It adds up, doesn't it?

TONY: I'll bet you're right, I'll bet that's it.

BRANDEN: What odds will you give me?

Family Life

Did your parents project that they believed in your intellectual and creative potentialities? Or did they project that they saw you as mediocre or stupid or inadequate?

Client: Jack, twenty-two years old.

BRANDEN: What's your initial response, Jack?

JACK: Definitely negative; both parents put me down.

BRANDEN: Okay, go ahead, talk about it in detail. What specifically happened?

JACK: Well, take my folks separately. First, my mother.
I remember once my mother was helping me study for a test. We were sitting on the bed together, and she was shooting questions at me for a history class. I was in the sixth grade at the time. I couldn't remember the name of a particu-

lar historical figure, even after she told it to me twice, and on the third time I got the name backward, so instead of calling him Richard Stevens, I called him Steven Richards, or something like that. Anyway, she began to scream and holler at me—she always was terribly impatient with me if I didn't get things right immediately, and she would shout and yell at the top of her lungs, always asking what was the matter with me and stuff like that. She would never hesitate to reproach me in front of other people and to bring up old mistakes and to tease me and make fun of me, always intimating what a burden I was and a dunce and so forth.

If I had a school essay to do, a paper of some kind, and I wasn't right on top of it immediately, she'd take over and do it for me and complain, "I've got to do it for you again." She was always doing my papers for me. She would never let me do them or not do them as I wished—and take the consequences if I didn't do them or do them right. And she always conveyed an enormous resentment that I was putting this burden on her. It made me feel pretty crummy and very frustrated.

BRANDEN: What else did it make you feel?

JACK: Fear.

BRANDEN: Fear of what?

JACK: Fear of her anger, fear of being hit or slapped, which she did all the time. Fear of her exploding at me. Now I'd like to tell you about my father.

BRANDEN: Okay.

JACK: My fear of my father was worse. Mother would have her ups and downs, sometimes she would be in a good mood and sometimes in a bad, but Father was more steady, more constant, and more frightening for that reason.

I used to enjoy writing—English composition, writing poems—and also painting. Father ridiculed that, didn't think it was important. He kept stressing the importance of math, and kept telling me how I absolutely must excel at mathematics the way he did. He would ridicule my artistic interests all the time, as though they were negligible or worse than negligible—unmanly—and what was wrong with me that I leaned in that direction. I did very well in English initially, then I began to do badly at it; then one summer I went away to prep school and again I got an A in English; then I came back home, resumed regular school in the fall, and began doing badly again. The same thing happened later when I went to college. I could only do well when I was away at school and not seeing my family. I couldn't take the pressure at home.

I remember when I was eleven years old and I was playing Ping-Pong with my father and I lost and got somewhat upset over it, and my father told me, "You pick any subject or field you want, just name anything at all, and I'll beat you at it, I can do better than you at everything." He told me that more than once.

Whenever I said anything or did anything he didn't like, he would always say, "You're stupid." He spoke to everyone in the family that way, not just to me. He would tell my mother and sisters they were stupid, too, anytime they said anything he didn't agree with.

Sometimes, I would stand under the shower and

call him a son-of-a-bitch at the top of my voice—
no one could hear me, of course—and afterward
I would feel better for awhile. I never got all the
rage out, just a little bit of it.

I really felt crushed by him, and intimidated and
frightened. He always gave me the feeling that
I'm nothing.

My mother's shouting at me leveled off somewhat after the time I tried to kill her.

BRANDEN: Tell me about that.

JACK: I was, oh, I don't know, fourteen or fifteen at
the time. I was working on some project for
school, which entailed cutting out various pic-
tures from magazines and so forth to illustrate ...
to provide illustrations—you know the kind of
thing they make you do in school?

BRANDEN: Sure. Go ahead.

JACK: Anyway, I needed a picture of the Taj Mahal.
My father took me to a store where we found a
book and we brought the book home, and I was
working at a table, and my mother was sitting on
the sofa a few feet behind me. She saw me
cutting this picture out of the book and when she
asked my father how much the book cost, he told
her that it cost nine dollars. She swung a book at
me and it hit me in the back—I was startled out
of my wits. Aside from the fact that it hurt like
hell, I was really shocked. I jumped up, grabbed
her by the throat and told her, "If you ever do
that to me again, I'll kill you." My father grabbed
me and pulled me away and began beating and
punching me. But anyway, after that my mother

didn't yell at me, or not so loudly as she had before; it seemed to quiet her down a little.

Back to my father. He would help me with math problems, but if I didn't understand something after he had explained it a couple of times, he would get up very impatiently and tell me, "I don't have more time to spend on this," and go off to watch television or something. He would often say, "I don't have time." He was very impatient with me.

When I would complain or express my frustration, or displease him in any way or challenge him about anything, his answer, which I heard again and again was, "I purchased you. I own you. You're my possession."

There was never any interest in what I was feeling or why I felt it. Neither of them would ever ask me why I got mad or upset. All that mattered was what they felt—above all, what my father felt. His feelings and wishes were supreme: no one else's mattered—certainly not mine.

I was stupid and a failure to the extent that I didn't live up to his expectations, do what he wanted me to do, think what he wanted me to think, and so on. That idea was conveyed constantly.

There was no patience with me, no sympathy, no understanding, no real effort to stimulate me or help me develop, none of that.

Oh, yeah. One other story I've got to tell you. Once, when I was eighteen, I brought a girl to the house. I was crazy about her. After she'd gone, my father's first words were: "Oh, come on, you can do better than that."

BRANDEN: What do you feel were the effects of all this on your psychological development? In other words, what conclusions were you drawing from these experiences, perhaps wordlessly? Are you able to identify anything?

JACK: Fear of my parents. Tremendous fear of both of them.

BRANDEN: What else?

JACK: A feeling that not to know something is the worst thing that could happen, the worst thing in the world. I mustn't admit I don't know something or the roof will fall in. I mustn't make a mistake, I mustn't make an error of judgment—it will be a disaster if I do.

BRANDEN: That attitude wouldn't be very conducive to your healthy intellectual development, would it?

JACK: No.

BRANDEN: Go on. What else?

JACK: Tremendous anger at my parents, which I wouldn't dare express for fear of retaliation. They'd really kill me if they knew the things I was feeling. So I had to bury it all.

BRANDEN: What else?

JACK: Guilt. The feeling that I should be studying, that I should be doing better in school, that I should be making my parents proud of me. But also a feeling of bitter satisfaction when I did poorly, the sense that I was getting back at them, frustrating them, not being the kind of son they wanted.

BRANDEN: But the desire to please them is still very strong in you.

JACK: Oh, sure. Like they're inside my head, demanding things all the time, and I can't escape.

BRANDEN: They're inside your head, all right, no question about that.

JACK: Whenever I'm with my father I'm feeling: What is he going to ask that I won't be able to answer? What will he expect me to know that I don't know? I no longer feel that just with my father, but with any adult. I constantly have that tension with people, especially older people.

BRANDEN: Go on.

JACK: If I want to make a proposal at work or even a simple suggestion, I think it through two dozen times, as scrupulously as I possibly can, because I'm in terror of somebody finding fault with it.

BRANDEN: Aren't you rather intellectually overcautious generally?

JACK: Probably.
When I do talk to people at work, or make suggestions, I'll often talk just like my father, in his tone of voice, or using one of his phrases. The staff has noticed this and commented on it to me many times. "You're just like your father." I hear

that often. Since my father is president of the
company, I. . . .
My stomach is really getting knotted up. I must
be getting angry.

BRANDEN: We've noticed that before. When you begin
talking about your parents, the rage begins to
surface, and in the next second you have pains in
your stomach.

JACK: I know.

BRANDEN: You'll always have those pains, until you get
it all out.

JACK: Probably.

BRANDEN: You never really thought about your parents, did you?

JACK: What do you mean?

BRANDEN: I mean judged them—judged their way of
behaving, judged their way of treating you,
judged their values and their view of life.

JACK: No, I got angry at times, but that was all.

BRANDEN: You accepted and internalized their values.

JACK: Yes. I can often hear my father inside my head
when I'm thinking about something. He's always
there.

BRANDEN: That must be very difficult for you.

JACK: It is.

BRANDEN: What are you feeling right now?

JACK: This is funny. I'm feeling sorry for my father. He wanted to do his best by me—he always wants to do his best at everything—but he just didn't know how. I didn't realize that when I was younger. I thought all parents were like mine; I thought all parents hit and screamed at their children. Now I know what a failure he's been. I mean, a failure as a parent—he's very successful at his work. And now I feel sorry for him. I've never seen him cry; but sometimes when I'm disappointing him in some way, he looks very frustrated and I know he wants to cry, because he doesn't know what to do, but he won't let himself.

BRANDEN: I wonder who you're really feeling sorry for right now—your father or yourself.

JACK: I never think about myself, only about what my parents or other people expect of me. It's really weird.

BRANDEN: We hear so much about the alleged virtue of selflessness. I want you to understand how vicious the concept really is. Look at yourself—because your psychological state is what that concept really means. What you have to learn is *selfishness*—the reclaiming and reassertion of your own ego. We have a lot of work to do.

The Dropout

In your parents' expectations concerning your behavior and performance, did they take cognizance of your knowledge, needs, interests and context? Or were you confronted by expectations and demands that were overwhelming and beyond your ability to satisfy?

Client: Leonard, twenty-five years old.

BRANDEN: The expectations and demands that I'm inquiring about, Leonard, may pertain to any aspect of human activity. They may be principally of a moral nature: they may involve satisfying some ethical code. Or it may be a matter of obtaining high grades in school. Or performing well at athletics. Or executing various tasks around the house.

LEONARD: My father was a Baptist minister. *Is* a Baptist minister.

BRANDEN: Go on.

LEONARD: He was very strict. Very quick to condemn. Very stern. Very concerned that I always act in such a way as to be a credit to him, that I never do anything the neighbors might consider unbecoming in a minister's son.

BRANDEN: What kind of things were you cautioned never to do?

LEONARD: Never raise my voice. Never masturbate. Never fool around with girls. Never speak disrespectfully to elders. Never shout. Never get in fights. Never laugh too loud or make too much noise.

BRANDEN: And your mother? What was her position?

LEONARD: She went along with Dad. Also, she was very concerned with school. That interested her the most. I had to get high grades. Neither of them cared about sports or things like that. I didn't, either. I was on the small side. Afraid of fights. Not good at athletics. I was always very nervous.

BRANDEN: Did you feel able to satisfy your parents' expectations?

LEONARD: Not entirely. I always felt very unsure and insecure. I never knew what my father might take as a violation of his rules; it wasn't always easy to predict. Also, I thought he was a hypocrite, because in his private life he didn't practice many of the things he spoke about in church. He was very bad-tempered and could be mean. And yet sometimes he was very kind. I don't know. It's confusing.

BRANDEN: What's confusing?

LEONARD: What to think of him.

BRANDEN: How do you mean? What's the problem?

LEONARD: I admired him in a way. He has a kind of strength, I guess. But he scared me a lot. I sort of loved and feared him.

BRANDEN: Did you feel he made an effort to understand you?

LEONARD: Not really, but I think that was because he was sure he did understand me and didn't have to work at it. In other words, he thought he knew what little boys were and I was a little boy, so what special thought did I require? That was his view, I believe. But he didn't understand me.

BRANDEN: Why do you say that?

LEONARD: He never noticed that I sometimes wouldn't understand the words he used. He warned me against "evils" and I wouldn't know what he meant, and he never seemed to notice. I didn't feel very real to him.

BRANDEN: Did you feel able to follow his moral rules?

LEONARD: I was interested in finding out what little girls looked like. I took a couple of girls into the woods and got them to take down their pants. I felt that was wrong and I felt I was bad. Then, I

had a lot of fantasies of hurting people. There
was a lot of hatred in me. I was scared all the
time.

BRANDEN: Of what?

LEONARD: I don't know. Scared that God would see
me and punish me. Scared that Dad would be
able to read my thoughts. Scared that I would be
hit.

BRANDEN: By whom?

LEONARD: By anybody.

BRANDEN: What about your school work?

LEONARD: I did okay in school, but not great—not
good enough to satisfy my mother. I just didn't
care.

BRANDEN: What do you mean?

LEONARD: Didn't seem to matter. I couldn't make
myself work harder. I had no energy.

BRANDEN: Can you describe how it felt to you at the
time?

LEONARD: An immense sense of weight. ... An emotional dullness, if that's the way to put it. ... If
she wanted to yell, let her yell.

BRANDEN: I wonder if this isn't the phenomenon we
talked about that afternoon when several of the
people in this group asked me how to derepress
childhood experiences and I had the idea of

these questions. Do you remember? The phenomenon of the child who goes on strike psychologically against pressures, expectations, demands that he feels he can't possibly satisfy. So he doesn't try to, he doesn't struggle, he doesn't rebel, he just——

LEONARD: He just says to hell with it.

BRANDEN: Exactly.

LEONARD: That's me.

BRANDEN: He just goes limp.

LEONARD: That's right.

BRANDEN: But you never pulled out of it. You're still limp. You're still passive.

LEONARD: I can't seem to make myself do things. I procrastinate all of the time. I never study until the night before an exam, and I'm often late with my papers. I almost never get things done on time. I just sit and daydream. Or go to the movies or do anything except what I'm supposed to do.

BRANDEN: What about a situation where it's a matter of pursuing a goal of your own, not an assignment for school. Do you behave any differently?

LEONARD: It doesn't seem to make the slightest bit of difference. Even if it's something I really want to do and it's for pleasure, a goal of any kind pressuring me to do something is upsetting. That's why I'm not getting anywhere.

BRANDEN: Let's go back to childhood for a minute. Close your eyes. Let your body relax. Take a long, slow, deep breath. You're nine years old. You're alone with your father and he's berating you for some moral infraction. You've done something to disappoint or anger him. He's speaking to you sternly. What do you feel?

LEONARD: Nothing.

BRANDEN: Are you afraid?

LEONARD: Yes. No. I don't know.

BRANDEN: What thoughts go through your mind as he speaks to you?

LEONARD: Playing in the forest, being away from him, out of reach. . . . I hate him.

BRANDEN: What else?

LEONARD: Feeling it's no use, there's nothing I can do.

BRANDEN: If you actively try to satisfy him, you just feel more anxious.

LEONARD: Yes.

BRANDEN: It's easier to give up.

LEONARD: If I'm bad, it's not so frightening. I mean, if I give up, if I accept the fact that I'm bad, I don't have to be afraid of being told I'm bad.

BRANDEN: Then you just resign yourself.

LEONARD: And not hope that he'll ever love me.

BRANDEN: Let your eyes remain closed, and slowly come back to the present. Take two deep breaths. That's right. Let your body relax. Now imagine that it's a few weeks before an exam. You know you should spend the evening studying. You're sitting in your room, thinking about it. What do you feel?

LEONARD: I don't want to be screamed at.

BRANDEN: Who's screaming at you?

LEONARD: My mother. Let her drop dead.

BRANDEN: Okay, open your eyes. You do get the point, don't you?

You don't know how to live up to your parents' expectations; you felt you could never satisfy those expectations, but you felt incapable of rebelling openly, or of challenging the validity of their demands.

You accepted your parents' position in that you took the blame, you damned yourself, you felt you must be in the wrong. You had to find a way to protect yourself within that context. So you became passive, you stopped struggling, you stopped expecting anything of yourself. You used resignation as a protective device, to make life bearable. You withdrew into a shell. You're still in that shell. You're afraid to come out of it. What might someone demand, you feel, that you'll be unable to do? So you're still in hiding, and probably hating the world, inside your shell.

LEONARD: That afternoon, when you explained this to us, I never related it to myself. I didn't really see how it applied to me.

BRANDEN: Do you see it now?

LEONARD: Sure.

BRANDEN: Unfortunately, we have to conclude at this point. We'll try to carry it further next time.

"We Poor Sinners"

Did your parents' behavior and manner of dealing with you tend to produce guilt in you?

Client: Susan, thirty years old.

BRANDEN: What's your initial reaction to this question, Susan?

SUSAN: Any time I did anything wrong—broke a vase or did poorly in some subject at school—Mother would ask, "Why are you doing this to me?"

BRANDEN: Elaborate on that.

SUSAN: She took everything personally, as though it meant I didn't love her or I wanted to hurt her. She made me feel awful. My father died when I was a few months old and my mother never remarried. I was brought up by her alone. She was always playing the martyr.

BRANDEN: How do you mean?

SUSAN: She would talk about how difficult it was for a woman to bring up a child alone, what a dirty blow fate had dealt her. But it always came across as though somehow it were my fault. She never said so, but that's what I took it to mean, and that's what I felt she was really telling me.

BRANDEN: What sort of things did she reproach you for?

SUSAN: Anything. Everything. Tearing my blouse. Being late for dinner. Making too much noise. Breathing. Anything. My grandfather, my mother's father, was a Lutheran minister. He gave me a lot of guilt, too.

BRANDEN: In what way?

SUSAN: "We poor sinners do confess unto Thee that we are, by nature, sinful and unclean and that we have sinned against Thee in thought, word and deed. . . ." Are you familiar with that?

BRANDEN: Sure. Or sentences like it. In the Wednesday afternoon group, I have a son of a Baptist minister, and he's talked of similar teachings.

SUSAN: I heard it all the time from my grandfather. I was reciting it from the time I was four years old.

BRANDEN: What did it make you feel?

SUSAN: Well, in a way, it made sense out of the guilt I was getting from Mother, as though guilt were my natural condition, as though guilt were everyone's natural condition, so there is nothing to protest about.

BRANDEN: Did that really make sense to you?

SUSAN: That's hard to answer. The whole question of "what made sense" wouldn't have come into my mind. It would have been foreign to our household, you might say.

BRANDEN: Let's pause on this. That answer isn't good enough. Whether or not you questioned what you were being taught, I don't believe the brain could absorb those teachings without any convulsion of protest whatsoever. Do you understand?

SUSAN: There were convulsions, I suppose. No, not convulsions—more like little ripples that came and went.

BRANDEN: Leaving behind—what?

SUSAN: Sadness.

BRANDEN: What else?

SUSAN: Guilt.

BRANDEN: What else?

SUSAN: Fear.

BRANDEN: What else?

SUSAN: Hatred.

BRANDEN: Of whom?

SUSAN: Of mother. Of grandfather. Of everyone. Of the world. Of myself.

BRANDEN: Why of yourself?

SUSAN: Because I existed. Because it's wrong to hate people. Because—I don't know.

BRANDEN: Try harder.

SUSAN: It just wears me out, even thinking about it, let alone talking about it.

BRANDEN: Force yourself.

SUSAN: I wanted to shout, "Why are you doing this to me?"

BRANDEN: But no one would have understood what you meant.

SUSAN: Exactly.

BRANDEN: There was no one to hear.

SUSAN: That's right.

BRANDEN: You must have felt very lonely.

SUSAN: I've never felt anything but lonely all my life. I don't know how to relate to people. I've never been able to keep a boyfriend.

BRANDEN: What happens?

SUSAN: I always do something to lose him. I sense at times that I do it deliberately, too, knowing I'll feel terrible afterward.

BRANDEN: What do you do?

SUSAN: Oh, anything. Pick a fight over nothing. Become irritable. Become critical. Act as though he bores me.

BRANDEN: Do you have any feeling about what drives you to do it?

SUSAN: No.

BRANDEN: You answered that so fast, you didn't even give yourself a second to think. Let me ask it again. Do you have any feeling as to what drives you to act as you do?

SUSAN: I don't want the man to leave me.

BRANDEN: Why should he leave you?

SUSAN: Because I'm a worthless human being.

BRANDEN: So you break with him before he can break with you.

SUSAN: Yes.

BRANDEN: What does it make you feel—to know that?

SUSAN: Nothing.

BRANDEN: Doesn't it make you feel worse about yourself?

SUSAN: Yes.

BRANDEN: Then come on, Susan, wake up and join this conversation. You're fighting me. What for?

SUSAN: I'd like to write a book. I'd have plenty to say about the so-called benefits of a religious up-bringing.

BRANDEN: I wish you would.

SUSAN: I suppose it's nothing new to you.

BRANDEN: It's not new to me, but that doesn't make it any less horrifying.
I've always been opposed to religion on philo-sophical grounds—I've been an atheist since the age of twelve. But it's since I began doing thera-py that I've been much more passionately op-posed to religion. I see its victims every day. I feel as though I am fighting for your mind—or your soul—against your mother, against your grandfather, against the whole vicious doctrine of guilt you began absorbing with your first breath.

SUSAN: I wish you luck.

BRANDEN: I'm not going to have any luck—not with you—if you intend to remain this passive and joke about it.

SUSAN: I feel it was too late for me since I was five years old.

BRANDEN: That's too easy. Much too easy.

SUSAN: That's how I feel.

BRANDEN: Fine, and I'm glad you told me. But that feeling is wrong, it's nonsense: you mustn't act on it or accept it as valid.

SUSAN: What difference does it make?

BRANDEN: You want me to value your life more than you do?

SUSAN: Yeah. I guess I'm testing you.

BRANDEN: I know you are. It won't work and we can't get anywhere—if I value your life but you don't. It's not a battle I can fight without you.

SUSAN: You know, I've never really done anything terribly wrong in my life, not really. Isn't that funny?

BRANDEN: No.

SUSAN: I've often felt tempted to, but I've actually never gone ahead and done anything I really thought was wrong.

BRANDEN: If that's true, then it makes your guilt the more tragic. But it isn't entirely true. You've done one thing wrong that I know of.

SUSAN: What?

BRANDEN: You've never actively thought about the things you were taught as a child. You were and are mentally passive.

SUSAN: That's true.

BRANDEN: That's your real guilt.

SUSAN: Strangely, that thought makes me feel better.

BRANDEN: Why?

SUSAN: Because if it's something I did—or didn't do—then it's still in my power, it's my own action. Then I can choose to act differently. I can change things.

BRANDEN: If you understand that, we've made real progress.

SUSAN: There's something else I feel. Saying these things makes me feel more kindly toward my parents. As though not saying these things all these years blocked whatever love I do feel for them.

BRANDEN: Of course. That's the way it works.

SUSAN: There were better times with them, happier times. It wasn't always bad.

BRANDEN: I'm sure it wasn't. It's repressing those negative feelings that keeps them alive. Releasing them permits you a clearer perspective, not only on your own life but also on your parents.

SUSAN: They're human beings, too. They have their own problems.

BRANDEN: They, too, had parents.

SUSAN: Yes. You're not saying they're blameless?

BRANDEN: No. But I want you to be realistic. Realistic about your own faults—and theirs. It's too easy to walk away from here saying, "My parents are to blame for everything."

SUSAN: I won't do that.

BRANDEN: Fine.
Shall we move on to another question?

Time Travel

Did your parents' behavior and manner of dealing with you tend to produce fear in you?

Client: Lillian, thirty-nine years old.

BRANDEN: Well, Lillian, in your case I know the answer already. It's obviously Yes. But let's talk about the details, let's talk about how it happened.

LILLIAN: My father believed that instilling fear was crucial to raising a child properly. It didn't happen accidentally; it happened intentionally and he went at it systematically.

BRANDEN: In what way?

LILLIAN: First of all, fear of God. "I'll put the fear of God in you"—I heard that sentence constantly from him. He meant it, too. It was important to him that I respond to his commands instantly; he resented ever having to say anything twice. If he wanted me to come in for dinner, he would say, "Lillian, come to dinner," quietly and ominously, and I'd better be there fast.

BRANDEN: Or what?

LILLIAN: He wouldn't hit me. He never had to. I think he liked the idea of controlling me just with his glance, with his eyes and with his voice. That was frightening enough. When he called, I came.

BRANDEN: What about your mother?

LILLIAN: Mother was too frightened herself to frighten anyone else.

BRANDEN: Frightened of him?

LILLIAN: Terrified. Of him and of anybody and everything else. I don't know which came first—fear of him or fear of the world.

BRANDEN: You must have been affected by her fear, too.

LILLIAN: This is strange. I've been thinking about this question all week—about the question of fear and my parents. I know I was afraid and I can remember many incidents. But I can't feel anything. I feel disconnected. Like it has nothing to do with me. I feel very remote, right now, in an odd way that's unpleasant.

BRANDEN: Describe anything you can about the feeling.

LILLIAN: I can recite story after story, if you like, things that happened—I think I have a memory for everything; the emotions are not even repressed, because I know what I felt, but I can't feel any of it now, I can't make any of it real except intellectually. As though it all happened to somebody else who my mind tells me was me.

BRANDEN: What do you feel in the present tense?

LILLIAN: Nothing.

BRANDEN: But a strange kind of nothing, a numb kind of nothing?

LILLIAN: Yes.

BRANDEN: All right, tell us of one incident that was especially frightening.

LILLIAN: Up until grade seven, I was a star student. I was always at the top of the class. Something went wrong in grade seven, I don't know what, but my marks dropped. I didn't fail, but they dropped to average. I remember walking home with my report card, petrified. I was special, I was supposed to be special, that's what Father always told me, I was to be the top of everything I did.

BRANDEN: What happened when you gave your father the report card?

LILLIAN: He read it, he looked at me, he told me to go to my room, without supper, and said that he would be up later to talk to me. I went up to my room and waited for him. It seemed like hours before he came. I have no idea how long it really was.

BRANDEN: And then?

LILLIAN: He came in and began to outline my "program" for the next three months. No parties, no movies, no going out in the evenings. He specified how many hours I was to study every day, after school, and what extra chores I was to do around the house when I wasn't studying.

BRANDEN: He didn't show any interest in trying to learn why your grades had dropped?

LILLIAN: No.

BRANDEN: He didn't actually reproach you?

LILLIAN: No. His whole manner was the reproach.

BRANDEN: Then what happened?

LILLIAN: Next thing I remember, he must have left the room; I heard Mother's voice talking to him downstairs and she sounded very upset and I could hear her shrieking but I couldn't hear what he was saying.

BRANDEN: What are you feeling right now?

LILLIAN: Nothing.

BRANDEN: Close your eyes. Don't try to feel anything, don't try to command your feelings. I'd like you to use your imagination. I want you to see that girl sitting in her bedroom, waiting for her father to come upstairs.

LILLIAN: I can't see anything.

BRANDEN: Don't rush it. Take several deep breaths and let your body relax. Let the scene come to you. It will come. Take your time.

LILLIAN: All right, I see her.

BRANDEN: Look at her. Look at her face. Look at the posture of her body. Forget what you know intellectually about how she feels. Try to read her feelings from her face and posture. Look at her eyes and her mouth. Try to understand what she is feeling merely from watching her. Good, you're getting it now. Now ... when you're ready ... when you really understand what she feels, from looking at her ... slip inside her body, enter her person, and look at the world through her eyes.

LILLIAN: Oh God, I can't stand it, I'm afraid, I'm so afraid. . . .

BRANDEN: It's all right, stay with it. You're feeling it now, aren't you? You're feeling everything.

LILLIAN: Yes.

BRANDEN: Go on feeling it, it can't hurt now, it's good for you—face it and know it all. We'll wait for you, take all the time you want.

LILLIAN: I don't want to open my eyes.

BRANDEN: What will happen if you open your eyes?

LILLIAN: I don't want to come back to the present with these emotions.

No, wait, something is happening. . . .

I can open my eyes now.

BRANDEN: Go ahead.

LILLIAN: Wow!

BRANDEN: You're not disconnected now.

LILLIAN: On, no. It's all real. That son-of-a-bitch.

BRANDEN: That's what he was, all right.

LILLIAN: He wasn't only a son-of-a-bitch. He could be marvelously generous at times. He would bring me presents unexpectedly. Take me for long walks.

BRANDEN: I know.

LILLIAN: It would be so much simpler if I could write him off as a total bastard and leave it at that.

BRANDEN: How are you feeling now?

LILLIAN: Much better. Calm. Peaceful.

GEORGE (another client): Could you explain what you just did?

BRANDEN: Sure. There's nothing mystical about it. It's very simple.

The fear was repressed, it was blocked off, because it was intolerable—or so Lillian felt. She was mistaken when she said she hadn't repressed

it. She had retained the factual knowledge of the
fear and made it impersonal, unrelated to herself, which is certainly a form of blocking or
repressing.

So we had to cut through that block. Ordering
herself to feel wouldn't do it. We had to approach the fear indirectly. We had to lead her
mental focus to the right point, the point where
the emotion would again be real and integrated
into her conscious experience.

So, first we chose the event, the time when she
brought her father the bad report card. Then we
move the camera in—think of her consciousness
as a camera—to focus on the little girl waiting in
her bedroom. Then we move in still closer, fo-
cusing on the girl's face. All of my suggestions
were intended to get her mind concentrated on
the girl's face and mood and to ignore everything
else, to forget about everything else, so that the
total of her perception was concerned only with
that. In other words, heightened concentration.

Now what is the little girl feeling? Let's find out
by looking directly at her, by interpreting the
meaning of her expression and posture. That
makes it more real, because empathy is demanded in order to do it. Lillian's defenses are down
now, the resistance is gone, because they aren't
Lillian's emotions, they're that little girl's emotions; it's someone else, but now Lillian begins to
feel with that someone else, to feel for her, to
really experience what the little girl is feeling.
Then, when she's fully experiencing empathy,
she enters that little girl's consciousness, she becomes that little girl, she becomes reunited with
her childhood self, and the past and the present
become integrated emotionally. And the disasso-
ciation is gone.

GEORGE: Why is she feeling better now?

BRANDEN: Lillian, can you answer that?

LILLIAN: I think so. Because at the same time that I'm letting the fear be real in the present, I also have the benefit of my present perspective and knowledge.

BRANDEN: That's right.

LILLIAN: It doesn't ... fill up everything or swallow everything—I think that's it ... the way it did then.

BRANDEN: Okay, the next step is to write a long paper accounting every distressing memory connected with your father that you can dredge up. I want you to tell me the story, in as much detail as you can remember, with special emphasis on the things you were made to feel. Naturally, I want you to discuss how you believe it affected your subsequent development. The standard assignment.

LILLIAN: Got it.

BRANDEN: Incidentally, you can use this technique I just showed you to help recapture the reality of what happened.

LILLIAN: I already thought of doing that.

BRANDEN: Okay, let's call it a day.

Togetherness

Did your parents respect your intellectual and physical privacy?

Client: Ellen, thirty-six years old.

BRANDEN: Ellen, let me explain what I mean by this question, in case it's not fully clear. This question might have been treated as a subcategory of the question about respect—because respecting a child's intellectual and physical privacy is one of the forms through which parents communicate respect for his person. Does a child feel free to keep a diary, if he wants to, without fear that it will be read by one or the other of his parents? Can he retire to his own room safely, knowing that no one will enter without knocking? These are the sort of issues we're concerned with here.

ELLEN: There was no lock on our bathroom door, and when I was eighteen years old neither of my parents would hesitate to enter while I was taking a bath.

BRANDEN: How did you feel about that?

ELLEN: I was furious.

BRANDEN: What did you say to your parents?

ELLEN: I protested. But it was useless. "Who do you think we are, strangers?" Mother would say to me.

BRANDEN: What other intrusions of your privacy were there?

ELLEN: If I had a girl friend over and she was visiting with me in the bedroom, we had to leave the door open. There was no such thing as a private conversation. Mother would very often pick up the extension when I was on the telephone, and I would hear her breathing when I was trying to talk to someone. When I complained, she would say, "What's the matter? Do you have secrets? Are you doing things you're ashamed of?"

BRANDEN: Go ahead. Anything else?

ELLEN: I would run to a field, near our house, just to be alone for awhile. That was my only escape. But as soon as I returned home, Father would ask: "Who were you with? What did you do?" Suspiciously.

BRANDEN: What did it make you feel?

ELLEN: That I was a prisoner, that I had no rights.

BRANDEN: Go ahead.

ELLEN: That I was helpless. That I had no dignity. That neither my mind nor my body belonged to me. I think my father was a dirty old man.

BRANDEN: Why?

ELLEN: He came into the bathroom too often when I was bathing. If I was doing anything else, I put a stool against the door, so at least I'd have warning. But it was nerve-wracking. I'm still nervous and tense if I'm alone in the bathroom, waiting for I-don't-know-who to burst in. I can't shake the feeling.

BRANDEN: Everything is public.

ELLEN: Family togetherness.

BRANDEN: Do you feel it affected your psychological development?

ELLEN: It, and a lot of other things. It was part of a wider pattern. I don't think I have a favorable answer to a single question on your list. Why do some people have children?

BRANDEN: Because they're "supposed to." Because they feel they have no other way to give their life meaning. Because they are nothing by themselves.

ELLEN: So they become something by torturing helpless children?

BRANDEN: What are you feeling right now?

ELLEN: I want to cry.

BRANDEN: That isn't all.

ELLEN: I guess I'm angry.

BRANDEN: At both parents, or one in particular?

ELLEN: Both of them. They deserve each other. But I didn't deserve either of them.

BRANDEN: Try to understand what happened between you and your parents, how their attitudes and behavior affected you. Let yourself know everything you felt and feel now, feel it fully and try to understand everything contained in the feelings. Without being blinded by hatred and self-pity on the one hand, and, on the other hand, without rationalizing your parents' behavior and finding excuses for everything they did. Do you think you can do that?

ELLEN: Yes.

BRANDEN: Try to relax. Think of all those invasions of your privacy. Think of what it made you feel. Just relax and let yourself reexperience that feeling. That's right. Thoughts will begin to come to the surface of your mind. Let them come.

ELLEN: That's why I can't say No. ....

BRANDEN: Go ahead.

ELLEN: If a man asks me to sleep with him. ....

BRANDEN: Keep going.

ELLEN: Who am I to refuse?

BRANDEN: You're not a person.

ELLEN: No.

BRANDEN: You have no rights.

ELLEN: No.

BRANDEN: Try to carry this further.

ELLEN: People can use me. Why not? I don't deserve anything better. I've never had anything better.

BRANDEN: It's all right. ... Let yourself cry. ... Don't fight it.

ELLEN: I don't want to be an object.

BRANDEN: You must learn to stop treating yourself as an object.

ELLEN: I feel such self-loathing.

BRANDEN: Do you? All the way down? There's nothing inside you that rebels against that?

ELLEN: I don't know.

BRANDEN: I do.

ELLEN: You don't see me as loathsome?

BRANDEN: I see you as a person fighting for her life. I want you to win.

ELLEN: You're the first person who's ever treated me with respect.

BRANDEN: If only you could be the second. . . .

ELLEN: Oh, God, Nathan! . . .

BRANDEN: Please try to think about it. You must. Okay, we'll rest here. That's enough for now.
I wish I could stay with this longer. But I have another group in an hour. To be continued.

Anti-Self

Did your parents project that it was desirable for you to think well of yourself, to have self-esteem? Or were you cautioned against valuing yourself, and encouraged to be humble?

Client: Norman, thirty-four years old.

BRANDEN: Before we get into this question, I want to say that I am very impressed with many of the papers I've been receiving from different members of the group. You all know how much importance I attach to the writing of papers. One of the things I'm most eager to teach in therapy is how to think psychologically, how to think about oneself and one's problems. Some of the papers contain excellent analyses of the impact of various childhood experiences on subsequent psychological development. It makes me happy to read them.

It's obvious to everyone, of course, that there's much more to solving problems than understanding their childhood origins. But still, for the kinds of problems we predominantly deal with in this group, and in my other groups, such understanding is vitally important.

Okay, Norman, are you ready? Let's go.

NORMAN: My mother was very fond of biblical sayings. She was quoting the Bible constantly. Two of her favorites were: "Pride goeth before a fall" and "Judge not that ye be not judged."

BRANDEN: Both of which injunctions are profoundly anti-self-esteem in their implications.

NORMAN: That's the point I'm making. It's kind of interesting, the attitude in our home toward pride. I would say my father was a proud man, in his own way. Not boastful or arrogant, but proud. But I don't think he would have regarded himself as proud or considered it desirable. My mother definitely would not have.

BRANDEN: What was your own attitude toward yourself as a child?

NORMAN: Not proud, that's for sure. The sense that I had so much to live up to—to be strong like my dad.

BRANDEN: What else?

NORMAN: I've done a lot of thinking about this. I have the feeling there's something very important in this question, but I can't quite get hold of it yet.

BRANDEN: Can you say anything about the area in which you think the importance lies?

NORMAN: An idea just came to me. I don't know what to make of it. A feeling of ... fear of succeeding ... fear of success ...; success is associated with pride. ...

BRANDEN: Try to describe the feeling.

NORMAN: Something terrible will happen to me.

BRANDEN: If you succeed?

NORMAN: Yes, I think that's it. If I rise too high. ...

BRANDEN: If you rise too high, what?

NORMAN: It's so difficult ... like it's in my mind, but I can't quite grasp it. ...

BRANDEN: Well all right, let's step back a bit. Consider why it's important to encourage the development of self-esteem in a child.

NORMAN: I think I understand that.

BRANDEN: A human being should value himself, should achieve self-confidence and self-respect.

NORMAN: I'd want to teach that to a son of mine. I'd want to teach him there's nothing to be afraid of.

BRANDEN: Nothing to be afraid of. ... How do you mean?

NORMAN: Here we are again, at that damn fear. You know, I've never considered myself particularly religious, but I'm beginning to suspect that I've underestimated the effect of religion on me in the early years.

BRANDEN: Can you say anything further about that?

NORMAN: Just the feeling that all that preaching by my mother did something to me.

BRANDEN: What did it make you feel? What was the net effect on you, emotionally? Are you able to say?

NORMAN: I have to be careful. If I reach the top. . . .

BRANDEN: Some kind of disaster will befall?

NORMAN: Yes.

BRANDEN: God will smite you down?

NORMAN: That's how it feels.

BRANDEN: Can you relate that feeling to your present problems?

NORMAN: I must conceal how well I can do things, I mustn't flaunt it. I mustn't really let go, use everything I've got, I mustn't stand out too much.

BRANDEN: Is that where your super-polite, super-respectful manner comes from?

NORMAN: Yes, I think so.

BRANDEN: God will be jealous of you?

NORMAN: I know it sounds ridiculous.

BRANDEN: No it doesn't. It has some serious meaning to you. That's what we have to understand.

NORMAN: I don't even believe in God.

BRANDEN: I know, but that's not the issue. I'm interpreting "God" metaphorically, anyway. What you're saying need not be taken literally.

NORMAN: I do believe I've absorbed the idea, longer ago than I can remember, that I must be humble. . . . And yet, I've always wanted to excel. . . .

BRANDEN: To live up to your father's expectations?

NORMAN: In part. But it hasn't only been that.

BRANDEN: No, of course not. You're a highly intelligent man. Intelligence cries out to be used. You want to use what you've got, you want to experience your powers.

NORMAN: Right. But I'm afraid to. Afraid to let go, all the way.

BRANDEN: Do you experience the origin of the problem as lying in those religious ideas your mother taught you when you were young?

NORMAN: That's the way it feels to me. I haven't thought of that aspect of my childhood in years. But working on these questions and thinking about my childhood in general brought these memories back to me . . . and now they keep persisting. . . .

BRANDEN: "Pride goeth before a fall." What do you take that to mean?

NORMAN: If you think you're good, something catastrophic will happen.

BRANDEN: And "Judge not that ye be not judged"?

NORMAN: The same thing. I know it doesn't literally mean that, but that's how I took it, I think, and what it means to me now. To judge—to be able to judge—means to trust yourself, to believe in yourself, to be sure of yourself, to consider yourself competent and qualified to judge.

BRANDEN: Which, in fact, everyone should be.

NORMAN: But the implication is that if others judge you—look out.

BRANDEN: Meaning, they'll find something terrible in you.

NORMAN: Yes.

BRANDEN: But suppose there is nothing terrible in you?

NORMAN: The Bible doesn't allow for that.

BRANDEN: And neither did your mother?

NORMAN: I guess not.

BRANDEN: In other words, we're all sinners in the sight of God.

NORMAN: Yes.

BRANDEN: Well I hate to disappoint your mother, but I don't think you're a sinner. I don't mean that you haven't ever done anything wrong; I'm sure you have, but that's not the point.

NORMAN: I know what you mean.

BRANDEN: You're not a sinner in the religious meaning of that word.

NORMAN: Why are you so sure?

BRANDEN: You think I'm mistaken?

NORMAN: Actually, no.

BRANDEN: I wonder if the retaliation you're afraid of—a retaliation for succeeding—is to come, not from God, but from your father. I wonder if that's the actual meaning of your feeling.

NORMAN: I always felt I could never be as good as he was.

BRANDEN: I know. That's part of what got me thinking along this line. And something else—fear of him is implicit in your whole attitude.

NORMAN: I admire him enormously.

BRANDEN: That doesn't negate the fear, does it?

NORMAN: I guess not.

BRANDEN: It looks as though we're not going to find the final answer today. We'll have to try again. It's there somewhere, and we'll get it.

NORMAN: I feel as though we're almost there.

BRANDEN: But there's a piece missing. You may have to go on and work with other questions on the list; I don't believe in staying with one question too long. Because sometimes we hit a block, we can only go so far, but then by pursuing another question, by attacking the problem from another angle, we get through the block and find what we're looking for. That's happened quite a number of times. So we'll give this a little more work at our next meeting, but if we can't solve it, we'll switch to another question.

NORMAN: This is really exciting—even if it's painful.

The Burdened

Did your parents project that what a person made of his life, and what you specifically made of your life, was important?

Client: Linda, thirty-one years old.

BRANDEN: Go ahead, Linda.

LINDA: My first reaction to this question is negative. Both my parents projected the idea to me that although one tries to get ahead, it won't really happen.

BRANDEN: Elaborate on that.

LINDA: Sort of . . . resignation to the fact that life is hard. It was as if my folks didn't think of "what you made of your life," but rather of "what life made of you." The person didn't have much to do with it.

BRANDEN: Could you give some examples of how this idea was communicated?

LINDA: That's a bit difficult. My father always talked negatively of one of my uncles—the one that was the most successful. He would imply that my uncle was stuck up ... above the rest of us ... "too good to get his hands dirty."

BRANDEN: Did you gather that your father resented success?

LINDA: I didn't think about it exactly, but, looking back, that's what it seems to have added up to, that's what I felt it to mean.

I don't recall talking about what I would be when I grew up. I didn't talk about such things to my folks or to anyone else. I think I just assumed—you know—girls grow up and get married and have kids. Hardly any of the women I knew worked when I was a kid.

When I was fifteen or sixteen I wanted to be a beautician. But my folks said it was too hard. You had to stand on your feet all day and put your hands in harsh chemicals and so on. They didn't want me to be a secretary either. Secretaries all went out with their bosses and slept with them, my dad thought.

BRANDEN: In many homes, parents project different attitudes to sons and daughters. Sons are more likely to be taught that it's important what they make of their lives, that it's good to be ambitious, to want to accomplish something; whereas girls are brought up to be—girls: appendages to the man, breeding machines, not encouraged to have

an identity of their own, not encouraged to be
ambitious.

LINDA: I can't say my folks projected a more positive
outlook on life for men than for women.

I think you'd have to enjoy life, or have some
hope of enjoying it some day, before you could
project the idea that your life and what you
made of it was important. But in my home, there
was this terrible, deadening resignation. My folks
never seemed to really enjoy themselves. They
never seemed happy. Nothing seemed to give
them pleasure. Life was a weight and a burden.

They never went anywhere without us kids.
They never had a life apart from us. When I
think of my folks, I think of them working all the
time and being tired and worn out.

My folks would talk about having a trade, about
my learning to be good at something, so that if
something happened to my husband—to my future husband—I would be able to support my
kids and myself.

BRANDEN: What did their attitude make you feel?

LINDA: Why try? You're not going to make it anyhow.
I always felt that. I thought I'd better try to
enjoy myself when I was young, because growing
up was growing up to misery and duty and end-
less, tiring work and no pleasure.

BRANDEN: Did you enjoy yourself when you were
young?

LINDA: I was pretty wild sometimes.

BRANDEN: Did you enjoy yourself?

LINDA: No.

BRANDEN: Do you feel their attitude got to you, got inside you—weighed you down, paralyzed you?

LINDA: It feels that way. I have no enthusiasm for anything. When I was younger, I went through a period of ... you know ... running around. But that was just an escape from loneliness and misery. It wasn't enjoyment.

BRANDEN: I wonder if you've ever stopped and thought about your life and asked yourself whether it really had to be the way your parents projected.

LINDA: If I did, I don't remember.

BRANDEN: You don't think about your life very much.

LINDA: I just try to get by, day by day.

BRANDEN: You don't plan ahead.

LINDA: What for?

BRANDEN: What do you feel right now?

LINDA: Resentment.

BRANDEN: Against me?

LINDA: As though I'm being pushed by you.

BRANDEN: Do you feel I'm reproaching you?

LINDA: I guess that's what it comes to.

BRANDEN: You have a bad conscience. Isn't your resentment hiding guilt?

LINDA: Yes. Sure.

BRANDEN: Describe how it feels.

LINDA: I don't want anyone else yelling at me or telling me what to do. I had enough of that when I was young.

BRANDEN: Your folks reproached you a good deal?

LINDA: All the time. Not really, but that's the way it feels.

BRANDEN: What do you want most in the world?

LINDA: I don't know. Not to have to work so hard.

BRANDEN: If you had more leisure time, how would you like to spend it?

LINDA: I don't know.

BRANDEN: You must feel dreadfully hopeless right now.

LINDA: I do most of the time.

BRANDEN: Do you think your passivity contributes to your feeling of hopelessness? Wouldn't your non-thinking and inertia serve to confirm your feeling that life holds no positive possibilities for you?

LINDA: Yes, I think so.

BRANDEN: You really let them defeat you, didn't you?

LINDA: My folks? I guess I did. I never thought of it that way.

BRANDEN: Think of it that way.

LINDA: I feel so sorry for my father today.

BRANDEN: Why?

LINDA: He's old, and he's sick, and he has no one.

BRANDEN: You've talked about letting him live with you. If you devote your life to feeling sorry for him and taking care of him, that will make your surrender complete, won't it? You'd have a perfect excuse to go on doing nothing. And you could even claim to be virtuous because of your self-sacrifice.

LINDA: I've already told myself that.

BRANDEN: Told yourself what?

LINDA: That it would be a weakness and an evasion to give up my life to him.

BRANDEN: Yes, it would.

LINDA: But I don't know what to do with my life. I can't seem to commit myself to anything.

BRANDEN: Of course you can't—if your basic premise is that you're doomed to defeat and failure.

LINDA: Do you think that I can get rid of that premise?

BRANDEN: I think you can. I don't know whether or not you will.

LINDA: Why?

BRANDEN: Unfortunately, I'm not certain you want to.

LINDA: Yes. I'm so tired.

Contagion

Did your parents encourage in you a fear of the world, a fear of other people? Or were you encouraged to face the world with an attitude of relaxed, confident benevolence? Or neither?

Client: Jerry, forty-two years old.

BRANDEN: There are at least two basic ways in which parents can instill fear in a child. One is to deal with a child in ways which the child experiences as frightening and threatening—the threat being the parents. We've talked about that.

But there is another way, subtler and more indirect. One or both parents may experience a high level of anxiety, and the child grows up in the atmosphere of this anxiety and begins absorbing it shortly after birth. Infants and children, as we know, are enormously sensitive and reactive to the presence of fear in their parents.

JERRY: This is a good question for me to work on because my parents certainly encouraged fear in me—fear of people and of the world.

167

BRANDEN: How was the fear transmitted?

JERRY: Until recently, I thought it came mostly from the emphasis at home on the dangers and disadvantages of being Jewish. I was told repeatedly that people would be against me because I was Jewish, whatever I did, whatever I attempted, and that I could only go so far in any field before I would be stopped.

By the time of my adolescence, I was feeling that I would not be able to accomplish anything in life. I became afraid of living from day to day. I couldn't picture myself doing any kind of work, not even the lowest, not even operating an elevator. I wouldn't be capable or confident. I wouldn't be able to handle it. It wasn't possible to accomplish anything, not for me. As a result, I began fooling around a lot in high school; I went to movies instead of classes, and my grades suffered.

BRANDEN: Do you still attribute your lack of confidence principally to fear associated with being Jewish?

JERRY: No. It goes deeper than that and began earlier. Anyway, as I grew older, I learned that the dangers they told me about in connection with being Jewish simply aren't true.

BRANDEN: No, they're not. Not in America. Sure, there is some anti-Semitism around—I encountered some of it when I was growing up—but not enough to matter, not enough to stop a person.

JERRY: I don't know why my parents were so hung up on that subject. Principally my father.

BRANDEN: Perhaps it was because they had deeper fears which they rationalized and attempted to make explicable in terms of anti-Semitism.

JERRY: When I was very young, I saw my father as a hero. I first associated fear with my mother. Her life was based entirely on what people thought of her. She was afraid of everyone; she was always worried about what people would think of her. If my sister or I, even when we were only five or six years old, brought friends home, Mother would be almost hysterical with fear that our friends would see some dust somewhere, that the house might not be absolutely neat and perfect—she was a meticulous housekeeper—and she became so upset about this that finally we stopped bringing friends home.

BRANDEN: You must have been breathing in her fear practically from the start of your life.

JERRY: I must have.

BRANDEN: That would be very hard for a young child to cope with. What else was she afraid of?

JERRY: That was the biggest fear. If she had to go to the market, her hair and clothes had to be perfect; if they weren't, she wouldn't go—we could all starve.
I don't recall being afraid of things before I was about nine. In fact, I was extremely fearless. I remember that in first or second grade, a big kid

picked on me and I threatened to hit him. I wasn't afraid of anything.

BRANDEN: What about your father?

JERRY: I didn't associate fear with him until recently, when I began to think about all this again. I remember how, when the doorbell rang and he was not dressed—he was only in his robe, say— Mother would get hysterical at the idea of someone seeing him like that, and he would run into the bedroom to hide. Then my sister and I used to hide, too, when the doorbell rang. When I was between eight and twelve, if the doorbell rang, I'd start to tremble, almost go into shock. I don't know what I was afraid of.

BRANDEN: Was there any talk in your home of the danger of burglars or things like that?

JERRY: Not that I remember.

BRANDEN: In what terms did they discuss danger?

JERRY: In part, as I said, it was the fear associated with being Jewish. There were some unpleasant anti-Semitic incidents in my life at that time, but although I used to think that was the main reason for my fear, I no longer think so.

BRANDEN: I take it your father didn't rise very high occupationally?

JERRY: No. He didn't use his Jewishness to explain that, but his lack of education. His father had been a compulsive gambler and, because of that, my father had to quit school and go to work at thirteen. As I grew older, I realized how fearful he was, and I lost my respect for him. He was terribly shy. Always very quiet with people.

BRANDEN: Didn't his shyness and fear carry the implication that people are frightening?

JERRY: Yes.

BRANDEN: How do you feel this all affected you?

JERRY: Very strongly. I seemed to absorb the fear. I remember Mother berating Father about refusing to shop for her when she only needed two or three items from the store. He felt people would laugh at him and think he was foolish for going to the store for just a few items. She berated him for being afraid of his own shadow.

BRANDEN: Often, people who are frightened themselves are enormously antagonized by fear in others: it increases their own anxiety.

JERRY: I became very afraid of people and the world. I got colitis, which is often the result of tension and fear, but I outgrew it later. If I was away from school a few days, due to sickness, I'd be terrified to go back, afraid to face anyone. I could never say what was so fearful. I'd force myself to go, but I felt almost physically paralyzed with terror.

BRANDEN: You grew up in an atmosphere of terror.

JERRY: Yeah.

BRANDEN: I have a feeling it was much worse than you remember, even now—and that it began much earlier. For instance, you first said that you didn't begin to feel fear until the age of nine, that until then you were fearless. But a few sentences later you remarked that by the age of eight you would be so frightened if someone came to the door that you would almost go into shock.

JERRY: That's true.

BRANDEN: How do you think this fear affected you in your relationships with people?

JERRY: I can remember being acutely afraid of people from my adolescence on. I was afraid even of relatives. Once, I went to the home of relatives for a wedding reception; I knew almost everyone there, but I was fearful of going, and after dinner I couldn't stand to have even the simplest conversational exchanges, so I went home.

I didn't date until I was in the service, and before that I thought I never would. I often crossed the street if I saw girls I knew, to avoid having to talk with them.
As I grew older, I saw myself as growing smaller and smaller, less and less worthy.

BRANDEN: I can suggest a reason for that. Let's assume you began absorbing this fear from infancy. It overwhelmed you and you didn't know how to cope with it. You began backing away from life, restricting your field of activity more and more, because of feeling helpless. But in backing away, you would only reinforce your feeling of helplessness; you would be continually strengthening your belief that the world was a frightening place and that you were incompetent to deal with it.

JERRY: I skipped school a lot, and my grades dropped, after being very good at first.

BRANDEN: Well, that would be an example of what I mean. You let the fear cause you to skip school, then you do poorly on your exams, then you feel strengthened in your belief that you're ineffectual and helpless, your self-confidence drops still further, the fear worsens, you feel less and less able to cope with life, you back away from challenges more and more, you reinforce your feeling of inadequacy and helplessness still more, and so on.

JERRY: That's what happened. By the time I was seventeen or eighteen, I couldn't imagine how I would function on my own—how I would support myself, even in the simplest, most menial job. I felt people would stop me from succeeding.

BRANDEN: You felt everyone else was ahead of you, was stronger than you, that they controlled the world you could never enter or succeed in.

JERRY: That's right. I quit high school when I was sixteen. The first beginning of confidence came in my job with the watch company; I did very good work and was praised by my boss. But even there, I had fits of anxiety; I would take off a day, then be terrified to go back. I'd wake up some mornings and feel I couldn't go on, couldn't face it.

At eighteen, I went into the service. That was a great psychological help; I felt I was on my own. I was in Communications. I saw that I could function and cope as well as other people, and perhaps better. When I went overseas, I had a pretty responsible job; I felt more responsible, felt more able to do things, and felt better about myself.

After the service, I went back to the watch company. I wanted to prove myself. I felt that I was a different person and I wanted to prove it. I was made a manager at the age of twenty; I held an important job, I did good work, deliberately shouldered extra responsibility. I began to acquire much more self-confidence.

BRANDEN: That was very good. You were determined to push forward and not surrender to despair.

JERRY: But the problem wasn't licked yet. Because later I moved on to a job at a hospital where I was attracted by the idea of the safety and security the job offered. I did good work there, but it was a job that led nowhere.

The real beginning of the breakthrough came only a few years ago, when I took on a much more demanding job with a publishing house. Things have been getting better since then.

BRANDEN: Are you able to say why they are getting better?

JERRY: Because I've been learning more and more about not letting fear stop me. Taking on things I know I have the brains to do, even if I'm scared.

BRANDEN: The fear has been diminishing?

JERRY: And continues to get less. When something makes me afraid, I just remind myself it's an old habit reasserting itself. It doesn't really apply to my present situation. I try to act against it and it goes away.

BRANDEN: There can be a justifiable pride in that— learning to face down fears until they disappear.

JERRY: That's what I'm feeling.

BRANDEN: One of the worst things parents can do to a child is to give him the impression that the world is terrifying, that people are threatening, that he's in danger simply by being alive. But the thing I wonder about is why, with your intelligence, your fear affected you as much as it did for so many years. I'm not satisfied yet. Not fully. There's more we have to find out.

You can be very pleased with yourself and proud, because you are moving ahead, you are growing, and you are defeating the fear. Still, let's see what else we can discover about the origin of the fear.

Armor

Were you encouraged to be open in the expression of your emotions and desires? Or were your parents' behavior and manner of treating you such as to make you fear emotional self-assertiveness and openness, or to regard it as inappropriate?

Client: Stanley, thirty-four years old.

BRANDEN: One comment before we begin.

I'm sure many of you have noticed that, often, the week after I work with someone on a question, he comes into group feeling very guilty about the things said about his parents at the preceding session. He feels he must talk about his parents' good points and minimize the negatives he discussed previously.

This is a mistake. I assure you that I am fully aware, as I sit listening to you, that you are telling us of only one aspect of your parents' behavior and of your relationship to them, and that it's not the whole story. Don't imagine that

the impression you leave me with is that your
parents are all monsters, with no redeeming
features.

Our purpose here is not to indict anyone for any
crimes, but to establish certain facts of your
childhood, as you remember them, and to explore
the impact of those experiences on your subsequent development. I know I've said this before,
but it bears repeating. If, when you're trying to
remember what happened, you are overconcerned
with being "fair" or "just" to your parents, that
can act as a memory-block; it can act as a
new agent of repression. We need to know what
you feel, whether it's justified or not, and what
you remember of your own childhood experiences, whether those memories are accurate in
every detail or not. In other words, we need to
know the meaning of your early life to you.
We're scientists or explorers here, not prosecutors
or juries. If we're to succeed in our investiga-
tions, you have to understand that and accept it.

STANLEY: That gave me trouble, at first, but not any
longer. I began thinking about these questions,
and I became very upset at some of the things I
was feeling about my parents. But now I've sort
of leveled off.

I had some trouble with this question on emotional openness. It's interesting that that's the one
we happen to be working on today. I find it hard
to answer.

BRANDEN: What's your initial response to the question?

STANLEY: Well, Nathaniel, I'm obviously very closed
emotionally. I find it very hard to show my feelings. Emotions embarrass me. Even other peo-

ple's emotions embarrass me. When some people began getting upset over these questions, and the memories the questions stirred up, I felt I wanted to run out of the office.

BRANDEN: Try to describe what you felt.

STANLEY: Nervous, out of control, anxious.

BRANDEN: We'll come back to that. But now, let's talk about your parents. Would you describe them as emotionally open or emotionally closed?

STANLEY: That's easy. Emotionally closed, both of them.

BRANDEN: What about anger? Did they or do they show anger?

STANLEY: No.

BRANDEN: You see, for many people who are emotionally repressed, anger is their sole emotional outlet. It's the only feeling they permit themselves to show. There's a principle I can give you here, by the way. Whenever you see a person whose sole form of emotional expression is anger, you can know that's a highly repressed person. Don't ever imagine that because he's free about projecting anger he's not emotionally repressed. Anger is merely the form in which his anxiety is erupting publicly.

STANLEY: I can never remember my parents showing anger. . . .

BRANDEN: You just thought of something.

STANLEY: Yes. I thought that they would consider anger in bad taste.

BRANDEN: Like any emotion?

STANLEY: That's right. That's right.

BRANDEN: When you were a young child, they never picked you up—you know, threw you in the air, laughed, openly showed excitement about you?

STANLEY: Not that I can remember.

BRANDEN: Do you remember them hugging or embracing you?

STANLEY: Occasionally. But they were very restrained. *Restrained* is a good word to describe them.

BRANDEN: When a baby is born, he doesn't know anything about "restraint." He begins by showing whatever he happens to feel. He learns certain forms of emotional expression from his elders, of course, but he doesn't start out wondering whether or not it's appropriate to show what he feels. If he feels it, he feels it.

STANLEY: That must be great—not to be afriad.

BRANDEN: Afraid?

STANLEY: It must be a fear of some kind that chokes a person up. I mean, chokes his emotions off.

BRANDEN: If a child begins inhibiting and repressing his emotional expression, that's the result of learning. It's an attitude or a policy he acquires.

STANLEY: How did I acquire it?

BRANDEN: Some parents behave toward their child in so frightening a manner that the child retreats from any form of self-assertiveness, including emotional self-assertiveness. He feels that any expression of his thoughts or desires places him in danger. That's a pattern of response we've talked about a great deal.

But there is another way a child can learn to inhibit and repress normal self-assertiveness. Reacting to his parents' lack of emotional responsiveness, reacting to their "restraint," as you call it, the child can wordlessly conclude that there is something wrong with being emotionally open, that it's inappropriate, socially "unacceptable." He learns to equate being "grown-up" with being emotionally closed.

STANLEY: That sounds like me.

BRANDEN: Yes, I think so.

STANLEY: That's right. When I see people being emotional, it always strikes me as immature.

BRANDEN: That depends on what you mean by "being emotional." Behaving irrationally under the pressure of emotions does represent a loss of control and is, in that sense, immature.

STANLEY: No, I don't mean that. I mean, showing eagerness, excitement, happiness, enthusiasm.

BRANDEN: That's not immaturity, that's self-confidence. That takes strength—as evidenced by

the fact of how few people retain the capacity
for such assertiveness.

STANLEY: When I read your chapter on emotions and
emotional repression in *The Psychology of Self-
Esteem,* I had an odd reaction, and I knew at the
time it was odd. I understood what you were
saying, I understood it intellectually, but I felt
cut off, as though it weren't really penetrating.

BRANDEN: Well, I think we can see why.

STANLEY: I feel like slowly, very slowly, something is
getting through to me today.

BRANDEN: Emotions proceed from our values. They
reflect our value judgments. To be ashamed of
our emotions is to be ashamed of our values, and
that means to be ashamed of our judgment. You
may not have thought of it that way, but that's
what it comes to. If we think something is good,
why should we have to conceal the fact? If we're
excited about something, what's wrong with
showing it? If we're happy, why should that be a
secret? Does that make sense?

STANLEY: No, it's ridiculous. But it's what I've done all
my life—hidden my feelings; not just my suffering, but all feelings, including pleasurable ones,
happy ones.

BRANDEN: It's impossible to repress only painful emotions. To repress painful emotions, one has to
repress one's values—the values that are being
frustrated or thwarted or negated. For example,
if a person wishes to repress the pain of loneliness, he has to repress the knowledge of how

much he values human companionship. But then, if he meets someone he can love and admire, he won't know how much it means to him; the knowledge will be repressed, and his love and happiness will be repressed also. Perhaps not entirely, but to a significant extent. The feeling will be blocked.

STANLEY: You know, I've been going with the same girl for two years. I've never been able to make up my mind whether I'm in love with her or not. I just don't know. I wonder if this is the reason.

BRANDEN: It very well could be.

STANLEY: Going back to when I was a kid, I can remember many times coming in to dinner, my emotions melting away as I got inside the house. I can see myself sitting at the dinner table, feeling very excited inside about something and making myself talk slowly, not showing any of my feelings.

BRANDEN: This took place before the age of ten?

STANLEY: Yes.

BRANDEN: Let me make a guess. In your late adolescence, I'll bet you can't remember any such occurrence. All such memories pertain to your early years.

STANLEY: Hey—that's right. What does that signify?

BRANDEN: A person doesn't begin, usually, by deciding to repress his emotions. At least, not in cases like yours. He begins by deciding to inhibit the outward expression of his emotions. He merely decides he won't show others what he feels. That's the first stage. But the second stage—and it's inevitable—is that the cut-off mechanism starts operating below the level of conscious awareness, so that it isn't merely the *expression* of his emotions that is blocked, but the emotions themselves. In other words, his knowledge of what he is feeling is repressed from conscious awareness. In the end, it's not only others who don't know what he feels; *he* no longer knows.

STANLEY: This could be my imagination, I could be crazy, but I can kind of see my mother wrinkling up her nose in distaste if I were really to show my emotions—I mean, any emotion, good or bad, happy or unhappy. And I can see my father looking in the other direction, as though he didn't know what to do.

BRANDEN: You're not crazy and I doubt that it's merely your imagination. If the thought occurs to you in this context, I would say it's valid.

STANLEY: Now that I really think about it. ... Yes. ... I'm sure of it, I'm sure they were that way.

BRANDEN: They're still living, aren't they?

STANLEY: Yes.

BRANDEN: What are they like today?

STANLEY: What's the matter with me? Of course: that's exactly how they are today.

BRANDEN: There's your answer.

STANLEY: So, in other words, they were signaling me ever since I was a baby, conveying the idea that one should be emotionally closed and unexpressive.

BRANDEN: It sounds that way, doesn't it?

STANLEY: I just thought—remember what I said a few minutes ago about being embarrassed by people's emotions? Just like my father.

BRANDEN: You noticed that.

STANLEY: Goddamnit, just like my father. How do you like that? But it's really inbuilt in me. It's hard to think of changing.

BRANDEN: You feel you must remain permanently cut off from yourself and from your own emotions?

STANLEY: I don't know.

BRANDEN: You feel you can't afford to remove your armor?

STANLEY: Armor?

BRANDEN: That's what it is, isn't it? What do you think that manner of detached remoteness is, except a way of protecting yourself against the disapproval of others? The condemnation of anyone who might not approve of the things you feel. Or who might not approve of your feeling anything.
But that isn't all that's involved. Your armor isn't merely to protect you from the disapproval of others. It's to protect you from any form of hurt. If you don't permit yourself to know how much

you want the things you want, you won't be hurt
if you don't get them. Or so you implicitly tell
yourself.

STANLEY: That rings a bell.

BRANDEN: Good.

CLYDE (another client): There's something I'm not
getting. Why is it anybody else's business what I
happen to be feeling? Why do I have to share
that with anyone who happens to be around?

STANLEY: Nathaniel's point is not that you have to
show everything you feel under any and all cir-
cumstances. There are times when we have to
ignore what we feel. Not repress it, but ignore
it—in order to do whatever it is we're doing. But
we should feel free about our emotions, free to
show and express them when appropriate.

CLYDE: Who is to say what's appropriate?

DENNIS (another client): Common sense tells you that.
You haven't shown any emotion since you've been
here.

STANLEY: Except annoyance, right now.

BRANDEN: A person's normal policy should be to be
open about the things he feels. Unless he has a
very specific reason not to. Under ordinary cir-
cumstances, why on earth should he not be free
to give objective emotional expression to his value judgments?

STANLEY: I'd like to get us back to an earlier point. Why does seeing other people's emotions embarrass me sometimes?

BRANDEN: Perhaps because the sight triggers off emotions in you, and you experience a loss of control.

STANLEY: I think——

CLYDE: There's another reason. If you equate showing emotions, or even having them, with being irrational, maybe you feel that if a person is in an emotional state he's dangerous, he might lash out and hurt you.

BRANDEN: Very good, Clyde. Are you describing yourself?

CLYDE: It just struck me.

STANLEY: Yeah, I think it describes me too. What both of you said. Both ideas seem to fit.

BRANDEN: They're not mutually exclusive. Many people equate emotions with irrationality. They believe that to feel an emotion is necessarily to be out of control intellectually—and therefore to be capable of doing anything, unpredictably and blindly. It's not true, of course. One can be feeling intensely and passionately and still be in full intellectual control.

Every mature human being is capable of that.

STANLEY: Boy, that's an idea that's going to take some getting used to.

BRANDEN: The place to begin getting used to it is right here, in this room. What are you feeling right now, for instance?

STANLEY: I don't know.

BRANDEN: Come on, Stanley.

STANLEY: I think I feel a little bit uncomfortable at being the center of attention for so long.

BRANDEN: What's wrong with being the center of attention?

STANLEY: Nothing. Everyone is looking at me.

BRANDEN: So?

STANLEY: Now I'm feeling ridiculous.

BRANDEN: Do you really not know that you're feeling good?

STANLEY: Am I?

BRANDEN: You're grinning. You're excited. You're feeling alive. You mean you don't know it? It's written all over your face.

STANLEY: Well, I feel as though something is opening up inside me.

BRANDEN: Is it a good feeling?

STANLEY: Yes.

BRANDEN: Then why don't you let yourself experience it fully? That's right, take a deep breath—and smile. There, you see? You're happy, you're showing it, and the world hasn't come to an end.

The Shame Mongers

Did your parents encourage you in the direction of having a healthy affirmative attitude toward sex and toward your own body? Or a negative attitude? Or neither?

Client: Gary, twenty-five years old.

BRANDEN: What's your response, Gary?

GARY: I think I would have to say "neither." I can't recall my mother or father ever uttering a word to me on the subject of sex.

BRANDEN: You feel they had no influence on your own attitudes regarding sex?

GARY: Not that I'm aware of.

BRANDEN: How would you characterize your attitudes today?

GARY: I've got hang-ups. I know I have.

BRANDEN: Such as?

GARY: A diffuse sense that sex is dirty.

BRANDEN: Try to develop that theme a little further.

GARY: Just a feeling ... not that sex is evil, more a feeling of distaste. ...

BRANDEN: How does that feeling affect you sexually?

GARY: It ties me in knots somewhat. I don't feel free. I don't feel natural. Very self-conscious. I really hurt my girl friend, because right after sex I usually have to take a shower. I can't wait. A compulsion.

BRANDEN: What else?

GARY: I don't enjoy going to bed that much. It's okay, but I'm missing something. Something is wrong. I feel so. ...

BRANDEN: What?

GARY: Constrained. Inhibited. Withdrawn.

BRANDEN: Let's return to your parents now. What—

GARY: I don't know what to say.

BRANDEN: What did your parents project toward each other? What can you infer about their own sexual attitudes?

GARY: I never saw any of that.

BRANDEN: Never saw anything between them that suggested the relationship of a man to a woman?

GARY: Not in the sexual sense.

BRANDEN: No kissing or embracing?

GARY: It's impossible to think of my parents kissing and embracing. I want to laugh.

BRANDEN: Why?

GARY: It's so unthinkable.

BRANDEN: Talk about that.

GARY: Well ... it's as though they'd never heard of sex.

BRANDEN: They had you. They must have heard something.

GARY: I think I must be an immaculate conception.

BRANDEN: If that's the way it feels to you, doesn't that say something about your parents' attitude toward sex? Doesn't that tell you anything?

GARY: You mean, the absence of any suggestion of a man-woman relationship between them?

BRANDEN: Exactly.

GARY: I never thought of that. Yeah.

BRANDEN: Yeah, what?

GARY: If sex was something not to be made real between them, then it's not a normal, natural part of life. It must be something to be hidden.

BRANDEN: You do see that?

GARY: I see it now.

BRANDEN: You never asked them any questions about sex?

GARY: Not that I remember.

BRANDEN: What about—

GARY: I just thought of something.

BRANDEN: Go ahead.

GARY: When I was little, my mother and father . . . especially my mother . . . it's coming to me now . . . I really felt there was something disgusting about having to go to the bathroom. I don't remember how it started. I remember feeling that. They were very shy and uncomfortable about it. I saw that many times. But there's something else, something I can't get hold of. . . .

BRANDEN: Something earlier in your life?

GARY: I . . . think so.

BRANDEN: Do you have any memories of being bathed by your mother?

GARY: I remember my father watching once, from a doorway, when Mother was cleaning me. He had an ugly look on his face.

BRANDEN: Try to describe it.

GARY: Not anger. Like finding an insect in your soup. That kind of look. I don't have any more memories, but I can feel that revulsion, I have the sense of that revulsion coming from them, from both of them, I'm sure of it. Isn't that odd? I can't remember, and yet I do remember something.

BRANDEN: You have that emotional impression.

GARY: Definitely.

BRANDEN: Then I think it's reasonable for us to assume it's based on something real.

GARY: I feel sure of it.

BRANDEN: What did it make you feel?

GARY: My genitals are dirty, foul.

BRANDEN: You don't think you're projecting that—after the fact?

GARY: It's too real to me now. I can feel it. It can't be a projection. I'm sure of it.

BRANDEN: Okay, we'll accept that. You must realize that the child's first sex education begins with the view of his body projected by his parents. That view can be projected by the way the parents handle the child, by the way they bathe him, deal with his bathroom functions, and so forth. They can project a natural, accepting attitude toward bodily functions and a healthy, affirmative attitude toward the body, or they can project an attitude of distaste, a negative attitude. Do you see what I mean?

GARY: Very clearly.

BRANDEN: Do you feel you began absorbing a highly negative attitude very early?

GARY: There isn't any question about it in my mind now. That's my earliest sense of myself as a physical being: something to be ashamed of.

BRANDEN: You're conscious of feeling that shame now.

GARY: Yes. I could have outgrown their view, I suppose, but I didn't.

BRANDEN: You probably never gave the issue any real thought.

GARY: Yes.

BRANDEN: That's the trouble. That's always the trouble.

I want to tell you something.

I went for a walk this evening, before group. I was thinking about all the stories that have been told during the past few weeks. We've learned a lot about how many of the problems began—some of the historical roots, anyway. Understanding by itself, of course, isn't enough. You all know that. The big job still lies ahead: changing your attitudes and ways of functioning as adults. Historical understanding makes you more intelligible to yourselves, and I don't wish to minimize the value of that, but we all know that "insight" isn't enough. Without action, without conscious, volitional changes of behavior in the present, changes in thinking processes and changes in action, there's no growth, no real improvement. So that's the next step.

As I was walking tonight, I felt I wanted to come here and say to all of you: "Life is so simple, life can be so wonderful, there's so much to do and achieve and experience. Forget all your nonsense. Forget what somebody did or told you twenty years ago. Why should any of that matter now?" I'm not even sure it's good strategy for me to be saying this to you. I don't want this to turn into another occasion for you to feel guilt.

GARY: It *is* the thing to say. It doesn't make me feel guilty. It makes me feel good. Because right now, at least for this moment, I understand what you're saying. And my hang-ups seem stupid and senseless to me, too. If only I could feel that way tomorrow.

BRANDEN: That's the battle. That's what we have to achieve.

The End
and the Beginning

*Did your parents' manner of dealing with you
tend to develop and strengthen your sense of your
masculinity or femininity? Or to frustrate and diminish it? Or neither?*

Clients: John, twenty-six years old; Elizabeth, twenty-
eight years old; the entire group.

BRANDEN: It's been a long road, but here we are. The
last question.

JOHN: We've hit every aspect of child-parent relations
there is.

BRANDEN: No, we haven't. Not by a long shot. But I
believe we've covered the major categories. I can't
think of anything fundamental we've omitted.
With one possible exception.
I'm thinking of the terrible value vacuum in
which most children grow up. The absence of
rational ideals or standards in the views commu-

nicated by their parents. The absence of anything or anyone to admire. The boring mediocrity of the vision of life handed down to most children by most parents.

What does that value vacuum do to a child? How does it affect his development? Especially when, with very rare exceptions, he won't encounter anything better in the world around him, when he grows up. As many of you know, I regard the works of Ayn Rand as the one major exception to this value vacuum in the field of literature.

There are really two aspects to this issue. One is the absence of rational, uplifting values to inspire the child. The other is the absence of human beings the child can admire.

Psychologists speak a great deal about the importance of the child's need *for* love. They don't talk nearly enough about the child's need *to* love. Children want so desperately to respect and look up to their parents, and they're so often frustrated in this desire; or they feel themselves able to achieve it only by deceiving themselves about their parents, by not really looking at their parents, not really judging them—which generates its own problems.

Okay, enough. John, let's go to work.

JOHN: The person whom I feel is most relevant here is my father; I would say he diminished my sense of my own masculinity. I came home after a fistfight once, obviously the loser, and my father took it personally. He demanded that I go back and continue the fight. He had false ideas about masculinity—all the mistakes we've talked about in group. He was very rough and very physical. He never gave me any encouragement, was never warm or affectionate. He wanted his sons to be just like him: rough, tough—you know.

BRANDEN: Go on.

JOHN: His only form of emotional expression was physical roughness. That was his affection. If I came into the house and I wanted something from him—some contact, some acknowledgment—my first impulse was to become physical, to wrestle or box.

BRANDEN: With your father?

JOHN: I wasn't very good at it, but he could relate to that, at least.

BRANDEN: Tell us more about his attitudes.

JOHN: My father didn't understand my feelings about sex. We lived near a red-light district, and he implied that I wasn't a man because I didn't go to a whorehouse to get laid. He even offered me money to go to the whorehouse. He got hurt when I refused the money; felt insulted.

BRANDEN: What did he say?

JOHN: All I can remember is that he acted disappointed. I would try to please him in other ways. I had a false sense of masculinity. I thought it meant to be coarse, to swear, to talk rough.
My father used to get pleasure from telling about his sexual acts, his adventures. I thought that to be a man meant to act like an animal.
But when I tried it, that didn't work.

BRANDEN: How do you mean? Physical fights?

JOHN: No. I always hated those.
     One night, at dinner, he asked me if I smoked
     and I told him I did. I was copying him. He
     slugged me and sent me to my bedroom.

BRANDEN: How old were you?

JOHN: I was twelve. We lived in New Mexico. I
     hated growing up. I formed the opinion that life
     was not a pleasure, but just misery.
     My father taught me that a real man knows how
     to bluff. I bluffed my way through many situa-
     tions: bluffed my way through fights; bluffed my
     way into jobs; bluffed with girls, trying to get
     them to fall for me, acting phony, acting like a
     big man.

BRANDEN: What did that make you feel?

JOHN: Small.

BRANDEN: You felt you were a fraud.

JOHN: I still feel that way.

BRANDEN: Because you act tough, but know you're not?

JOHN: Yes. And because I can't live up to my father's
     expectations; that makes me feel bad, too.

BRANDEN: Makes you feel you're not a man.

JOHN: Yes.

BRANDEN: What about your mother? Do you think she influenced your views concerning masculinity?

JOHN: I don't know. I can't think of anything. I'm only aware of my father.

BRANDEN: What kind of woman is your mother?

JOHN: A nice woman. Quiet. Dominated by my father. Subservient to him.

BRANDEN: You feel your sense of yourself as a man was crushed by your father.

JOHN: Overwhelmingly. I can practically see him sneering at me right now. "Look at the punk."

BRANDEN: That must be very painful.

JOHN: Excruciating.

BRANDEN: I'd like to do something a little different today. Instead of continuing straight on with you, John, I'd like to hear from a woman at this point. Is there a girl here who would care to tell us about the impact of her parents' attitude on her sense of femininity?

ELIZABETH: May I talk?

BRANDEN: Sure.

ELIZABETH: I don't consider myself as feminine as most women. I still tend to be tomboyish. I think of myself that way, and sometimes I wish I were the other way, but not enough to try to change.

BRANDEN: Go on.

ELIZABETH: My mother was like me: athletic, enjoyed the company of men more than women, very intelligent. She was not a feminine woman; she was not my father's idea of a woman.

BRANDEN: You feel you're like your mother?

ELIZABETH: Definitely. My father was upset because I was interested in boys' activities. He thought girls were supposed to wear dresses. When I was in high school, if I wore slacks and a boy came over to the house, my father would make me change. His idea of femininity is frilly dresses.

BRANDEN: It sounds like yours is, too.

ELIZABETH: Well, I like my mother.

BRANDEN: But you don't think she's feminine. And you think you're like her.

ELIZABETH: It's a conflict.

BRANDEN: Can you tell us anything about it?

ELIZABETH: I went to a girls' school where we were taught that young ladies should not engage in athletics. We were supposed to be interested in home economics. I hated dealing with girls. They seemed so silly. They were boring. I was lousy at sewing, but I loved mathematics. Girls weren't supposed to like mathematics.

BRANDEN: Who said so?

ELIZABETH: I just got that feeling. I can remember wishing that I wasn't a girl.

BRANDEN: If you accepted the conventional view of femininity as meaning helplessness, non-intellectuality, non-ambitiousness, passivity, you would revolt against femininity. You would revolt against your nature as a female.

ELIZABETH: Yes.

BRANDEN: And yet, one can't really be happy revolting against one's sexual nature. One can't, with impunity, repudiate one's self. If you're a girl, you want to feel that you're feminine.

ELIZABETH: Yes, that's right. I felt caught, I didn't know which way to turn, didn't know what to do. I wanted a career; I wanted to accomplish something. But I wanted to fall in love with a man, too. And according to my father, men don't like intellectual, ambitious women.

BRANDEN: Usually it's the mothers who pass on that lovely message to their daughters.

ELIZABETH: Well, with me, it was my father.

BRANDEN: I hope you realize, today, how vicious and nonsensical that idea is. Sure, there are men who feel that way. Men with inferiority complexes. Men too unsure of themselves to want a woman to be strong and independent. But no woman in her right mind would want that kind of man anyway. And there are men who don't subscribe to the conventional view of femininity. Men who recognize that a woman is a human being and

that she has a mind and that she should use it.
Men who value strength in a woman.

ELIZABETH: I try to tell myself that.

BRANDEN: If a woman accepts a fallacious notion or
standard of femininity by which she judges herself to be deficient, the consequence is that she
will tend to act in unfeminine ways which will
then reinforce her initial negative self-concept.
She'll be tense and uncomfortable with men, perhaps belligerent, or emotionally closed, or sexless;
and then, as a consequence, she'll elicit negative
responses from men—and the problem will grow
worse.

ELIZABETH: Have you been spying on me?

BRANDEN: I don't have to. It fits?

ELIZABETH: It fits.

BRANDEN: The same thing applies to masculine self-
doubt, of course. If a man feels that he is unmasculine, or doubts his masculinity, he'll tend to act
in an unmasculine manner—and provoke responses from women that will confirm and worsen his
self-doubts. He'll be timid, or indecisive, or inade-
quately assertive, or childish, or belligerent, or
something else equally inappropriate.

JOHN: You're not kidding.

BRANDEN: It's appalling how unpopular intelligence is.
Did you ever think of that? In our culture, many
boys are encouraged to feel they're unmasculine
if they're intelligent, or if their intelligence is too

conspicuous—if they'd rather read books than engage in fistfights. And girls are encouraged to
believe they're unfeminine if they've got brains—
if they don't regard sewing and homemaking as
the ultimate fulfillment of their intellectual potentialities.

ELIZABETH: A lot of men fear intelligence in women.

JOHN: And a lot of women equate masculinity with
muscles.

BRANDEN: And a lot of people are irrational. But just
because they're crazy, do you have to be? Our
culture is filled with absurd notions concerning
the nature of masculinity and femininity. Notions
that cause people torment and self-doubt.

JOHN: Hearing Elizabeth gives me a clear insight into
my own past. Parallels. . . .

BRANDEN: You do see that.

JOHN: It's obvious.

BRANDEN: You know, while we've been working on
these questions during the past several weeks, we
really haven't functioned as a group. There has
been very little group interaction. I've been
working with one person at a time, to show you
how to use these questions, and aside from an
occasional comment or two, most of you have
remained silent most of the time, as the situation
more or less required.
Now I'd like to open up this discussion. I want to
stay on the subject of masculinity and femininity,
but I want to invite your comments—the com-

ments of everyone here—on this question. I think you'll find it illuminating.

If you were a mother or a father, raising a son or a daughter, what would you want to do to aid and encourage the development of healthy masculinity in your son and healthy femininity in your daughter? In what way do you think you might be able to contribute to their development?

RICK: Do parents have to do anything? I mean, if kids are left alone, won't they develop healthily and normally by themselves? What is there to teach them about masculinity or femininity?

BRANDEN: What do you people think about that?

MURRAY: I think there are things you can teach a child that would be helpful.

BRANDEN: Such as what?

MURRAY: Well, let's see. ... Encourage your son or daughter to have self-esteem.

BRANDEN: Right you are. Any time a parent does anything to encourage a child's self-esteem, the parent is indirectly encouraging a development of healthy masculinity or femininity. Self-esteem is the foundation. A person who lacks self-esteem, who lacks a sense of personal worth, cannot have a healthy sense of sexual identity—cannot feel properly masculine or feminine. Murray, that's a good beginning. We'll just go around the room in order. Gayle, what are your thoughts on this question?

GAYLE: This was suggested to me by what John was saying. If I had a son, I wouldn't let him feel that he's obligated to be interested in sports. If he is, fine. If he isn't, that's fine, too. I wouldn't make him feel it was a duty. I wouldn't want him to feel that he wasn't a real male if sports didn't interest him. That's his choice. And I wouldn't be shy or squeamish about explaining "the facts of life." That goes for a daughter, too. I wouldn't treat sex as a dark, dirty secret. Oh, yes, and if she wanted to climb trees, I'd let her climb trees. What the hell! I climbed trees. So what? What's so unfeminine about that?

BRANDEN: Nothing whatever.
Masculinity and femininity are concepts pertaining to sex and sex-related attitudes, feelings, and activities. It's incredible how few people seem to understand this. Is it necessary to point out that climbing a tree is neither a sexual nor a sex-related activity? Neither is working at mathematics, or sewing, or reading books, or enjoying art. Yet people drive themselves crazy over such activities—wondering about the implications for their masculinity or femininity.

BILL: I'd want to project a positive attitude toward the child's body. To encourage in a child a healthy, positive, unashamed attitude toward his or her own body.

BRANDEN: That's right. Masculinity or femininity entails an affirmative attitude toward one's sexual nature and one's sexual role. That includes an acceptance of one's physical being. A guilty or self-rejecting or self-repudiating attitude toward one's body necessarily undercuts masculinity or femininity.

KAY: My mother was ashamed of her body and she passed that shame on to me. I could feel it even in the way she handled me. Or the way she looked at me when I didn't have any clothes on. Like there was something wrong with nakedness. A naked body is awful; that's what she felt.

BRANDEN: Is there anything else you can add?

KAY: I'd want to attack the idea that femininity means helplessness; that's something else I was taught. Mother drove me crazy with that. I'd want to fix something that was broken, but I wasn't supposed to. I had to wait for Daddy. That was man's work.

ANDREW: This has already been said, perhaps, but here's what I'd want to stress. To me the most important thing is to communicate to the boy or the girl that sex is good, sex is clean—sex is a wonderful thing. I wouldn't want any fear or guilt associated with it.

BRANDEN: No one who reacts negatively to the phenomenon of sex, or to his or her own sexuality, can enjoy a strong, unimpaired sense of sexual identity, a happy and guiltless enjoyment of one's own role as a male or female.

ANDREW: I was given the impression that women were something to be afraid of. I wouldn't want my son to get that idea.

MURRAY: Or that women are just objects to be used.

ANDREW: That's right. That's no good either. I'd want to communicate. . . . How would you communicate it?

BRANDEN: What?

ANDREW: I don't know how to put it. That women aren't frightening mysteries, and they aren't just objects to be used.

BRANDEN: That they're human beings?

ANDREW: And that one should like them and feel comfortable with them.

BRANDEN: Don't you think that how you treated your wife would be very pertinent here? So much of the way we teach children is by example.

ANDREW: Yeah, that would do it.

BRANDEN: Ray?

RAY: I grew up to see kisses as a sign of duty, something demanded by my mother. I didn't get enjoyment out of it. I formed the idea that expressing affection is for women. I'm still hung up on that. I'd want my son to accept the expression of affection as being properly masculine.

If my child had physical defects—too short or overweight—I wouldn't bug him about it. I wouldn't make him feel inferior physically. I hated it when my parents talked about the size of my nose as though I weren't in the room.

BRANDEN: Anything else?

RAY: I'd keep the kid away from religion. So he or she would be spared that crap, at least.

GAYLE: That doesn't exactly bear on masculinity or femininity. That's more a matter of protecting the child's psychological health.

BRANDEN: True. But it does pertain to masculinity or femininity insofar as religious attitudes tend to invoke fear and guilt about sex.

RAY: That's what I was thinking of.

BRANDEN: Sandra?

SANDRA: I want my daughter to feel excited about life. I want her to like herself and to like being a woman.

BRANDEN: How would you communicate that?

SANDRA: Well, I guess I have to get there myself first, don't I?

BRANDEN: If you don't really feel it, she'll know it.

SANDRA: I'd try to teach her not to be afraid of men. That's where my mother wrecked me. "Men are beasts." You know the kind of thing I mean.

BRANDEN: Sure.

LLOYD: I'd want my son and daughter to see me treating their mother with respect. I'd want them to see her treating me with respect. So they'd get a benevolent view of the relationship between the sexes. Not see them as enemies.

ANDREW: Yeah, that's good. Not see them as being at war.

GAYLE: It's awful when you see them tearing at each other—insulting each other, treating each other with contempt.

KAY: Or seeing your mother use sex to manipulate your father. It's disgusting.

JOHN: Or seeing your father act like a dictator just because he's a man—as though being a man confers the right to be arbitrary and high-handed and irrational and to hurl orders whether they make sense or not. And the woman has to obey because she's a woman. I hate that.

LLOYD: Let the kids see the parents openly expressing love and affection for each other.

BRANDEN: Very important.

RICK: This discussion is great. It makes the issues clearer than they've ever been to me before.

SANDRA: I'm getting mad at my mother all over again. And I've been feeling so kindly and understanding.

BRANDEN: Miriam?

MIRIAM: I thought of something. Not to be afraid of surrendering to the man in bed. Not to feel she'll be hurt. To look forward to it and enjoy it.

BRANDEN: I'm very impressed with all of you. Everything you've said has been pertinent.

I don't wish to get us into a theoretical analysis of
the nature of masculinity and femininity—there's
a great deal to be said on that subject that we
can't get into tonight—but I would like to summarize what you've been saying and perhaps add
a point or two.

But before I do, I'm very interested in what
you're feeling right now, if anyone cares to express himself.

BILL: I can't say why, I just feel good.

SANDRA: Talking about what I'd want to do for my
own child helps me, somehow, to understand my
own childhood better, and to feel less bound by
it—freer.

MURRAY: It helps you to cut loose.

BRANDEN: Good. That's what I wanted you to feel.
Okay, let's summarize.

I think it's clear that if a child is to grow up with
an unclouded sense of his own sexual identity, an
affirmative attitude toward his own body is essential. He should enjoy his body and his existence as
a physical being. Anything parents can do to
encourage such an attitude is to the good.

Next, of course, is the attitude toward the phenomenon of sex. One can't be healthily masculine
or feminine while feeling fearful or guilty or hostile regarding sex.

In today's culture, the child inevitably will encounter a great many fallacious notions concerning masculinity and femininity. The parents
should try to arm their child against those notions—such as the view that an interest in art is
unmasculine or an interest in mathematics is un-

feminine. There is so much of that poison around; parents should arm their children against it in every way they can.

The relationship between the parents is very important, as more than one of you has said. The parents should set an example by the way they treat each other. Let the child see emotional openness and love between his mother and father. Let him see that the expression of emotion is not unmasculine. That's one fallacy that's wrecked any number of men: the belief that expressing love or warmth is unmanly.

SANDRA: Will you tell that to my husband?

BRANDEN: Send him in, and I'll tell him.

Let the child see that men and women are not enemies, that the idea of "the battle of the sexes" is absurd. That the interests of men and women are complementary, not inimical.

Oh, yes, a point I should have made earlier, a point I should have begun with. It's something you seem to understand very well. Anything that encourages the child's self-esteem encourages the healthy development of masculinity and femininity.

Now here's something which I regard as of prime importance. One or two of you hinted at it, but it wasn't made sufficiently explicit. We've talked about enjoying one's sexual role as a man or a woman. That's part of it. If you're a man, not being afraid of the responsibility of masculine self-assertiveness. If you're a woman, not being afraid or inhibited about responding to the man, about surrendering sexually. That's what it means to enjoy one's own sexual nature.

But there's a wider issue involved here. This may not be a very elegant way to say it, but here's the thought. If I were a father, I'd want to convey to my son or daughter that, as a man, I think the existence of Woman is the most magnificent and exciting thing in the universe. The best idea Nature ever had. And if I were a mother, I'd want to convey to my son and daughter that, as a woman, I think the existence of Man is the most magnificent and exciting thing in the universe. The best idea Nature ever had.

SANDRA: That says it, N.B.

BRANDEN: Speaking literally, of course, I don't wish to imply that I regard the relationship between the sexes as more important than creative work. I don't.

MURRAY: It's perfectly clear.

BRANDEN: Perhaps this is enough for now. Shall we call it a night?

ELIZABETH: Can you tell us anything about the book?

BRANDEN: It's not a theoretical book. It's not intended to be. The theory is in *The Psychology of Self-Esteem*. I want to show what these questions mean, and how they can be used therapeutically. The book will be frustrating, in a way, because I won't be tracing the problems through to their solutions. I'll be showing one phase of the total process.

ANDREW: What are you going to call it?

BRANDEN: It will be a grim book. At one point I thought of calling it *Is This What Destroyed You?* But that's not the spirit I want to convey. I want a title that will sum up what's really happening here, what we're engaged in doing. I decided on the title only a few days ago. I'm going to call the book *Breaking Free*.

ABOUT THE AUTHOR

Also author of *The Psychology of Romantic Love*, *The Psychology of Self-Esteem*, and *The Disowned Self*, Dr. Nathaniel Branden lives in Lake Arrowhead, California and is in private practice in Los Angeles.

As Director of the Biocentric Institute in Los Angeles, he offers Intensive Workshops in self-esteem enhancement, man/woman relationships, and personal transformation, in major cities throughout the United States. He also conducts professional training workshops for mental health professionals in the Biocentric approach.

Dr. Branden has given lectures, seminars, and workshops in over fifty colleges, universities, and other institutions in North America and Europe.

He is now engaged in writing a new book.

Communications to Dr. Branden or requests for information about his various lectures, seminars, and Intensive Workshops should be addressed to The Biocentric Institute, P.O. Box 4009, Beverly Hills, CA 90213.